THE GREAT
BOOK OF OHIO

The Crazy History of Ohio with Amazing Random Facts & Trivia

A Trivia Nerds Guide
to the History of the
United States Vol.6

BILL O'NEILL

DON'T FORGET YOUR FREE BOOKS

CONTENTS

CHAPTER TWO
OHIO'S POP CULTURE 24

CHAPTER FOUR
FACTS ABOUT OHIO'S ATTRACTIONS.................. 70

CHAPTER FIVE
OHIO'S UNSOLVED MYSTERIES, URBAN
LEGENDS, AND OTHER WEIRD FACTS 93

CHAPTER SIX

INTRODUCTION

How much do you know about the state of Ohio?

Sure, you know it is home to Cleveland and the Ohio River. But, do you know how the state got its name? Do you know why its nickname is the "Buckeye State"?

Do you know which famous U.S. President was visiting the state when he found out he was elected?

Do you know why Ohio was sued over its state motto? Do you even know what its state motto is? Have you heard what makes the Buckeye State's flag unique?

Do you know which famous fast food chain got its start in the state? Do you know which childhood candy or which household cleaning tool was invented by Ohio natives?

If you have ever wondered about the answers to any of these questions, then you've come to the right place. This book is filled with stories and facts about the state of Ohio.

This isn't just any book about Ohio. It will highlight some of the facts that have helped shape the state's history and introduce you to facts you've never heard. Once you finish reading, you'll know everything there is to know about the state of Ohio.

Ohio is a state that's rich in history. We'll bounce around some as we take a closer look at some of the state's most interesting historical facts. We'll also explore the state's pop culture, sports, attractions, and so much more!

This book is broken up into easy to follow chapters that will help you learn more about the Buckeye State. Each chapter is followed by trivia questions and answers so you can test your knowledge on what you've just learned.

Some of the facts you'll read about are shocking. Some of them will give you goosebumps. But there's one thing all of these facts have in common: they're *all* interesting! Once you have finished this book, you're guaranteed to walk away with a wealth of knowledge about the Buckeye State.

This book will answer the following questions:

Why is Ohio called the "Buckeye State"?

Why is Ohio known as the "Mother of Presidents"?

Which superhero originated from the state?

Which famous children's book author got his start in

Ohio?

Which Ohio musicians went to high school together?

What fast food chains started out in the Buckeye State?

What urban legends haunt the state?

Which national sports league was formed in Ohio?

What Halls of Fame are located in the state?

And so much more!

CHAPTER ONE

OHIO'S HISTORY
AND RANDOM FACTS

Ohio was the 17th state to join the Union. Like most states, Ohio is rich in history. But how much do you really know about the state? Have you ever wondered where Ohio got its name? Do you know why it's known as the Buckeye State? Do you know which famous brothers were from Ohio? Have you heard about some of the state's most unusual laws? To find out the answers to these and other questions, read on!

How Ohio Got Its Name

Have you ever wondered where Ohio got its name?

Like many states in the country, Ohio's name originates from the Native Americans. Did you know Ohio actually got its name from the Ohio River?

The word "Ohio" originated from the word "Ohi:yo," which was the Seneca word for the Ohio River. "Ohi:yo" means "great river" or "beautiful river."

According to some translations, the word may actually mean "continuously flowing creek." This makes sense, as the Ohio River flows into the larger Mississippi River.

Seneca was the language spoken by the Iroquois Indians, who had settled in the Ohio River area in 1650. It's been estimated that only a few hundred Iroquois Indians have resided in Ohio during at any given time.

Ohio Didn't Officially Become a State Right Away

Almost every state has an interesting path to statehood, and Ohio is no exception. Did you know it took Ohio some time to formally become a state? Although Ohio was technically declared a state back in 1803 by Thomas Jefferson, it wasn't until Dwight D. Eisenhower signed and backdated Ohio's admittance to the union that things became official. Ohio's journey to statehood is a little more complex than that, though.

In order to become a state, territories were required to have 60,000 residents by the time they were admitted into the union. Back in 1801, Congress decided that Ohio's growing population—which consisted of 40,000 people at the time—was enough to allow it to begin the process to become a state. The Enabling Act of 1802 set Ohio's state boundaries.

In February of 1803, President Jefferson signed the act that approved Ohio for statehood. While Ohio was then recognized as the 17th state, the decision wasn't official yet. Due to an oversight, Congress didn't formally recognize Ohio's statehood in 1803.

In 1953, Ohio was formally declared a state by President Eisenhower. Today, it is still recognized as the 17th state, even though Louisiana technically was technically the 17th state to be formally admitted to the union.

Columbus Wasn't Even Formed When It Was Chosen as Ohio's Capital

Ohio's capital city was named after—you guessed it—Christopher Columbus! What's more interesting is that Columbus, Ohio hadn't even been built yet in 1803 when the state first unofficially joined the union. Columbus wasn't the state's first capital, either.

The original state capital was Chillicothe, Ohio. The capital was later moved to Zanesville and then back to Chillicothe in 1810. In 1812, Columbus (which was then the small town of Franklinton) was chosen as the state's capital because it was located within 40 miles of the center of the state. It wasn't until 1816 that the city of Columbus was actually formed.

Columbus has come a long way since it was formed. Today, Columbus is the most populated city in all of Ohio. With an estimated population of 879,170 as of

2017, Columbus is also the 3rd most populated state capital in the country (surpassed only by Phoenix, Arizona and Austin, Texas). Columbus is also 14th most populated city in the United States. It's also one of the fastest growing cities in the country.

The "Mother of Presidents"

Although Ohio has officially been nicknamed the Buckeye State, it's also often referred to as the "Mother of Presidents." This is because seven United States presidents were born in Ohio, and an eighth president lived in the state. The only state that has been the birthplace of as many presidents is Virginia.

The presidents who came from Ohio include:

1. **William Henry Harrison** – Harrison, who was born in Virginia, lived on a farm in Ohio until he was elected in 1836. He was the 9th President of the USA.

2. **Ulysses S. Grant** – Born in Point Pleasant, Ohio, Grant was raised in Georgetown. He served as 18th President of the United States between 1869 and 1877.

3. **Rutherford B. Hayes** – Hayes was elected right after Grant, making him the 19th American president. Hayes was born and raised in Delaware, Ohio. He served as president from 1877 to 1881.

4. **James Garfield** – Garfield served as the 20th President of the United States. Garfield was elected in 1881. He was assassinated the same year. Garfield was born in Orange Township, which is known as Moreland Hills, Ohio today.

5. **Benjamin Harrison** – Born in North Bend, Ohio, Benjamin Harrison was the grandson of William Henry Harrison. Benjamin Harrison graduated from Miami University in Oxford, Ohio. He served as the 23rd President of the United States from 1889 to 1893.

6. **William McKinley** – McKinley, who served as the 25th President of the USA, was born in Niles, Ohio. McKinley served from 1897 to 1901, when he was assassinated six months after his re-election.

7. **William H. Taft** – Taft was born in Cincinnati, Ohio and attended Woodward High School. Taft not only served as the 27th President of the United States, but he was also the 10th Chief Justice of the United States. He's still the only person in America who has held both positions.

8. **Warren G. Harding** – Harding served as the 29th President of the United States from 1921 until he died of heart problems and pneumonia in 1923. Warren G. Harding was born in Blooming Grove, Ohio and lived the majority of his life in rural Ohio.

Why It's Known as the Buckeye State

You probably already knew that Ohio is known as the "Buckeye State." There's even a candy named after it! But do you know how the state earned its nickname?

Ohio was given its nickname due to the buckeye tree, which can be found in the state. The Native Americans named the tree's nuts "hetuck," which translates to "buck eye." They chose this name because they believed the nuts resembled the eye of a male deer.

1. While the Buckeye tree is plentiful in the state and has even been named Ohio's official state tree, that's not the reason Ohio earned its nickname. The reason Ohio came to be known as the Buckeye State runs a bit deeper than that. When William Henry Harrison was running for president, his opponents painted a portrait of a man who was "better suited to sit in a log cabin and drink hard cider," according to StateSymbolsUSA.org. Harrison's supporters, however, used this to promote his campaign. Harrison became known as "the log cabin candidate." Harrison's campaign logo was a log cabin constructed of buckeye timber. His supporters also used buckeye canes in parades.

These campaign tactics worked out in William Henry Harrison's favor and he beat President Martin Van Buren in the election. Since then, Ohio has been known as the Buckeye State.

This Famous U.S. President Was in Ohio When He Learned He Was Elected

Abraham Lincoln was a Kentuckian, so it may surprise you to learn that it was while he was in the Buckeye State that he got the news that he'd been elected as President of the United States.

Lincoln was visiting with Governor William Dennison Jr. at the Ohio Statehouse back in 1861. It was there that he just so happened to learn that the Electoral College results were in and that he had been elected President of the United States.

The "Birthplace of Aviation"

Ohio is officially known as the "Birthplace of Aviation." This is because famous aviation brothers, Orville and Wilbur, were from Ohio.

While Orville was born in Ohio, Wilbur was born in Indiana. Both brothers lived and worked in Daytona, Ohio.

It was while the brothers were living in Dayton, that they built their first controlled machine that was able to fly into the air and then safely return to the ground. Orville and Wilbur Wright built the first practical airplane in history in 1905. It was known as the Wright Flyer.

Of course, Ohio's nickname of the "Birthplace of Aviation" has been widely debated, since many people feel that North Carolina is aviation's real birthplace. While the Wright brothers may have built planes in Ohio, their first successful flight took place in Kitty Hawk, North Carolina.

In 2003, however, Congress decided that Ohio was the official birthplace of flight.

Whether you agree with this decision or not, it's safe to say that aviation essentially started out in the Buckeye State!

A Famous Astronaut Was a Boy Scout in Ohio

Did you know that a famous astronaut was an Ohio native? Neil Armstrong, who was the first man to walk on the moon, was from Wapakoneta, Ohio.

Armstrong's love for flying also blossomed when he was just a child living in Ohio. When he was just two years old, his father took him to the Cleveland Air Races. Armstrong took flight lessons at the Wapakoneta airfield, earning a flight certificate at just sixteen years old—before he had even earned a driver's license.

While Neil Armstrong was growing up in Ohio, he was a Boy Scout. During adulthood, Armstrong was honored with the Distinguished Eagle Scout Award and the Silver Buffalo Award. When Neil Armstrong made his infamous flight to the moon, he greeted the Scouts. He also took a World Scout Badge to the moon and back!

A Historical Riot and Shooting Took Place at an Ohio University

One of the most historical protests and shootings of all time took place in Ohio. It took place when students at Kent State University were protesting for several days against the Vietnam War in May of 1970. While the protests started out peacefully, they turned violent, with students lighting the school's ROTC building on fire.

On May 4th, the Ohio state governor banned all political demonstrations. However, this didn't stop 3,000 students from protesting, cheering, and watching. The protestors were confronted by members of the Ohio National Guard with rifles, tear gas, and bayonets. Four students were killed and nine were injured that day.

Students across the country went on strike in protest of what had happened at Kent State University. Colleges and universities were temporarily closed, and the nation's public opinion against the Vietnam War began to become more unfavorable. Some even believe that the Kent State incident may have what been what caused President Richard Nixon to lose popularity among the American public.

Ohio Was Once Sued Over Its State Motto

Did you know that Ohio has been sued over its state motto, "With God All Things Are Possible"?

In 1997, Ohio was sued by the American Civil Liberties Union. The ACLU claimed that Ohio's state motto was in violation of the First Amendment, which grants American citizens freedom of religion.

However, it was determined that the motto isn't a violation of Americans' First Amendment rights. This is because the motto doesn't refer to any specific God. As a result, Ohio was given permission to keep its state motto.

A Historical College Can Be Found in Ohio

Did you know that one of the most historically significant colleges of all time can be found in Ohio? That college would be Oberlin College, which holds records for the following:

- The first college to ever admit African-Americans, as of 1835.

- The first college to ever admit women, as of 1837 when it admitted its first four female students.

- The first coeducational liberal arts college in the United States.

- The second continuously operating coeducational liberal arts college in the entire world.

- The first college from which a black woman earned a B.A. degree (Mary Jane Patterson in 1862).

Oberlin College is also considered to be one of the most LGBT-friendly colleges in the United States. If you're looking to go to one of the most progressive colleges in the country, then look no further.

This Surprising Talk Show Host Was Once Mayor of Cincinnati

It may surprise you to learn that before *The Jerry Springer Show*, Jerry Springer was the 56th Mayor of Cincinnati. It was back in 1977 that Springer was elected for the position. He was to only serve one year in office due to Cincinnati's political arrangements.

In 1982, Jerry Springer ran for governor of Ohio. Springer based his campaign on honesty, sharing the check he used to pay a prostitute. He did not win, however.

It was rumored that Springer considered running for Senate in both 2000 and 2004. He allegedly didn't follow through because he feared that the negative associations with *The Jerry Springer Show* would prevent him from winning.

One Ohioan Dialect May Surprise You

You might be surprised to learn that Southwest Ohioans have a dialect in which they share some aspects of their vowels with "northern New Jersey English." Like northern New Jersians, people from

Cincinnati are thought to over-pronounce their "O's," which results in a rounded "w" sound.

It has also been said that people in Southwest Ohio have some German influence on their dialect. One sign of this is that people use the word "please" when asking someone to repeat themselves.

Ohio is Known as the "Gateway State"

Did you know that Ohio is known as the "Gateway State"? This is, in part, because the state is home to the 10th largest highway network in the country. The state's geographic location makes it a prime location for people from the East to the West. It also is an important state for transporting goods and other resources.

Most people in the United States also live near Ohio! Research has also found that most Americans don't live too far away from the state. It has been estimated that approximately 60% of the American population lives within a 500-mile radius of Ohio, with an estimated 48% living within 500 miles of Columbus. This makes Ohio a prime spot for tourism.

Ohio is "The Heart of It All"

The shape of the state of Ohio is similar to a heart. This is what led to the slogan "The Heart of It All." This slogan was once frequently used to help promote entertainment, tourism, educational opportunities, and more.

Thanks to Ohio's central location, the state really *is* the Heart of It All for concerts, conventions, travel, and more. The state is a hub for sports fans. It's also an important state for healthcare, with the reputable Cleveland Clinic, as well as Columbus's Ross Heart Hospital.

RANDOM FACTS

1. Ohio encompasses 116,103 square miles. This makes it the 34th largest state in the country. As of 2018, the state was estimated to have a population of 11.69 million, making it the 7th most populated state in the United States. It's also been said that Ohio ranks as the No. 10 state that's most densely populated.

2. Cleveland, Ohio was the first city in the United States to ever receive electricity. The city was lit up by electricity for the first time in 1879. This is thanks to Charles F. Brush, a Cleveland resident who spent most of his life trying to understand electricity.

3. The first electric traffic light in America was implemented in Cleveland in August of 1914. The light, which was installed by the American Traffic Signal Company, was placed on the corner of Euclid Avenue and East 105th Street.

4. Akron, Ohio was the first city in the country to have ever used police cars. The first police car was used in Akron in 1899. The car, which cost a little over $2,000, was electric and was able to travel for 30 miles at a time. There weren't any high-speed

police chases going on in those times—the car could only hit 18 mph in speed.

5. The first speeding ticket in America was given in Dayton, Ohio. The ticket was given to Harry Myers in 1904. Myers was ticketed for going 12 mph on West Third Street.

6. The Great Flood of 1913 took place when the Great Miami River burst levees in Dayton, Ohio. It's been estimated that the death toll in Ohio was between 422 and 470.

7. Like every other state, Ohio has a lot of strange laws. If you're a woman, it's against the law to wear patent leather shoes in the Buckeye State. (This is so that men won't see the reflection of your underwear in them. Logical). It's illegal to go whale hunting in Ohio on a Sunday (and you probably won't catch much, since whales are now considered *extinct* in the state). It's also against the law to get a fish drunk. More than five women cannot legally live in a house. And if you've broken all of these laws? Don't worry. You also can't legally be arrested on a Sunday or the Fourth of July (though I don't suggest testing this one out since I'm pretty sure it's no longer practiced today).

8. America's first concrete street was built in Ohio! The street, which is located near the Logan

County Courthouse in Bellefontaine, was poured in 1891.

9. The Cuyahoga River has been nicknamed "The River That Caught Fire." This is because it has caught fire at least thirteen times—and that's only the number of times that those fires were documented. So, why so many fires? At one point, the Cuyahoga River was one of the most polluted rivers in the country. The fires would occur when sparks from the train fell into the river. The Cuyahoga River was cleaned up in 1969 but only after it received extensive media coverage.

10. The first professional and fully-paid fire department in the United States was established in Cincinnati in 1853.

11. In 1852, Ohio became the first state to establish laws protecting women in the workforce. Even though the legislature was passed, state authorities refused to acknowledge it for quite some time.

12. Ohio is home to the second largest population of Amish people in the country. As of 2017, an estimated 73,800 Amish people were living in the state. It was surpassed only by Pennsylvania, which had an Amish population of 74,300. Prior to 2010, Ohio had the highest Amish population in the United States.

13. The official state beverage of Ohio is tomato juice. This is because the Buckeye State is the second leading producer of tomato juice, surpassed only by California. Ohio is also one of the top states for tomato production.

14. Ohio's official state flower is the red carnation. This choice was a sentimental one. The flower, which was officially selected in 1904, was chosen to honor Ohio-born President William McKinley after he was assassinated in 1901. McKinley often wore red carnations in his jacket lapel.

15. The 4-H Club started out in Clark County, Ohio back in 1902. It was founded by Albert Belmont Graham, who was the superintendent of Springfield Township Schools. Graham organized the 4-H Club to teach school-aged children more about gardening and corn harvesting.

16. Presidential candidates work hard to win over Ohio voters. This is because Ohio is the *only* state to vote for every winning president in the last 50 years. This is why Ohio is a "swing state," as it's often one of the states that determines who will win the election.

17. The Ohio state flag has a pennant design. It's the only American state flag that isn't rectangular-shaped. A little-known fact about the flag is that it's meant to be folded 17 times to represent Ohio being the 17th state to join the union.

18. Many of Johnny Appleseed's apple trees were planted throughout the Buckeye State. He planted apples throughout much of Ohio. He gathered leather bags of dried apple seeds, which he had gathered from Western Pennsylvania cider presses. He crossed the Ohio River and planted his first apple orchard near George's Run, near Steubenville, Ohio.

19. Akron, Ohio was once known as the "Rubber Capital of the World." This is because Goodyear Tire & Rubber Company, one of the world's top tire producers, was founded in the city back in 1899. At one point, all four of the world's major tire-producing companies—Goodyear Tire & Rubber Company, Goodrich Corporation, Firestone Tire and Rubber Company, and General Tire—were all headquartered in Akron. A lot of jobs were provided by these companies for deaf people, which also gave Akron the nickname "Crossroads of the Deaf."

20. Thanks to glacier movement that took place in Ohio thousands of years ago, the Buckeye State has some of the most fertile lands in all of America. In addition to tomatoes, the state is a leading producer of soybeans. Other top crops grown in the state include corn, wheat, hay, oats, and popcorn.

Test Yourself – Questions and Answers

1. The word "Ohio" means what in the Iroquois' language?

    a. Great mountain
    b. Great river
    c. Great forest

2. A historical shooting took place at which of Ohio's colleges?

    a. Kent State University
    b. Oberlin College
    c. Ohio State University

3. Which United States President was *not* born in Ohio but lived in the state when he was elected?

    a. Benjamin Harrison
    b. William McKinley
    c. William Henry Harrison

4. Ohio has been called the "Birthplace of ____."

    a. Telecommunication
    b. Transportation
    c. Aviation

5. Nearly 50% of people live within a 500-mile radius of which of Ohio's cities?

    a. Columbus
    b. Cincinnati
    c. Cleveland

Answers

1. b.

2. a.

3. c.

4. c.

5. a.

CHAPTER TWO

OHIO'S POP CULTURE

Like most states, Ohio is a state that's rich in pop culture. Have you ever wondered what celebrities hail from Ohio? Do you know which famous music term originated from the state? Do you know which author was born in the state or which '90s boy band was formed in Ohio? Do you know which famous movie house you can tour in the state? Read on to learn more about pop culture in the Buckeye State!

The Term "Rock 'n' Roll" Was Born in Ohio

Did you know the term "Rock 'n' Roll" originated from Ohio?

The term was first used by a Cleveland disc jockey named Alan Freed. Freed apparently used the term to promote his own music during 1951, as well as the first rock show in Cleveland back in March of 1952.

His promotion was obviously a success! Since then, the term has been continuously used to describe this genre of music.

Knowing that "Rock 'n' Roll" got its name from Ohio, our next fact might not be too surprising.

The Rock and Roll Hall of Fame is Located in Ohio

Did you know the Rock and Roll Hall of Fame is located in Ohio? Although New York City was also considered as a home for the Rock and Roll Hall of Fame and museum, Cleveland was able to raise $65 million in public funding to secure it being built in their city. Of course, it only seems fitting that the Rock and Roll Hall of Fame be located in the city where the phrase was born.

Located in Cleveland, the Rock and Roll Hall of Fame is home to a number of exhibits related to rock 'n' roll. You'll find that the Hall of Fame, includes inductees ranging from the Beach Boys and Michael Jackson to the Beatles and Metallica.

Some of the things you'll find at the museum include the Power of Rock theater, an Elvis Presley exhibit, and artifacts including musicians' instruments, handwritten drafts of hit songs, and even pinball machines. You can also expect to find live music on occasion at the Rock and Roll Hall of Fame as well.

Superman Started Out in Ohio

Today, there have been a number of movie and television adaptations of Superman. But did you know that one of America's favorite fictional superheroes was born in Cleveland?

While they were attending high school in Cleveland in 1932, two students named Jerry Siegel and Joe Shuster became friends. That friendship turned out to be a match made in heaven. Siegel was an aspiring writer, while Shuster was an aspiring illustrator.

It was in January of 1933 that Siegel wrote and Shuster illustrated a story called "The Reign of the Superman." Siegel self-published the story in his fanzine, which was called *Science Fiction: The Advanced Guard of Future Civilization*.

Unfortunately, the fanzine didn't sell well and Siegel and Shuster switched to writing comic book strips for a while. Siegel eventually noticed that strips with heroes, such as *Tarzan*, began to grow in popularity. This led Siegel and Shuster to create Superman (who, surprisingly, had no connection to the character in the duo's first story).

The rest is pretty much history. By 1937, Siegel and Shuster had sold the copyright for *Superman* and it blew up into the success we know it as today.

It might surprise you to learn that Jerry Siegel and Joe Shuster didn't get rich off their creation. They didn't make millions of dollars as one might expect. They sold the rights to their idea for only $130. Once *Superman* blew up in popularity, Siegel and Shuster took the publisher of the comics to court. They each won $30,000 per year for life and were also awarded credits in future *Superman* movies and publications.

A Famous Filmmaker Was Born in Ohio

Did you know that famous filmmaker Steven Spielberg is from the Buckeye State? Spielberg has been called one of the "founding pioneers of New Hollywood."

Steven Spielberg was born in Cincinnati. While his family moved him to New Jersey when he was just four years old so his father could work at RCA and then later to Arizona.

Spielberg is one of the most popular filmmakers of all time. He was responsible for directing and producing films such as *Jaws, E.T. the Extra-Terrestrial, The Color Purple, Schindler's List, Saving Private Ryan, Jurassic Park,* and *War of the Worlds*.

Thanks to *Jaws, E.T. the Extra-Terrestrial,* and *Jurassic Park*, Steven Spielberg is the highest-grossing director in history.

Spielberg is also one of the co-founders of DreamWorks Pictures.

And to think it all started out in Cincinnati!

You Can Visit the *A Christmas Story* House Museum

A Christmas Story is one of everyone's favorite holiday movies. In fact, it's such a beloved film with a cult-like following that *TBS* airs it for 24 hours on Christmas. If you grew up watching the movie about Ralphie, who wants nothing more than a Red Ryder BB gun for Christmas, then you'll be pleased to learn that you can visit the museum in Cleveland, Ohio.

Situated in the original house that was used for exterior scenes from the movie, *A Christmas Story* House Museum encompasses three buildings and offers a number of things that may be of interest to fans of the movie. You can take a tour of the house and even spend the night! Inside the house, you'll find the iconic Leg Lamp from the movie.

Directly across the street from the house, you'll find a museum that contains a number of other artifacts from the movie. Some of these include Randy's snowsuit, the Parker family's car, Miss Shield's classroom chalkboard, and toys from Higbee's. There's also a gift shop where you can purchase *A Christmas Story* memorabilia, including your own Leg Lamp!

So, who is the owner of *A Christmas Story* House? It belongs to Brian Jones, a fan of the movie who bought the house on eBay for $150,000 back in 2008. Jones already owned a company called the Red Rider Leg

Lamp Company, which produces replicas of the lamp from the movie, prior to purchasing the house and the house across the street for the museum.

Other Movies Have Been Filmed in Ohio, Too!

While *A Christmas Story* might be the most well-known movie to be filmed in Ohio, it's not the only one. A number of other films have been shot in the Buckeye State. Some of these include:

- *Air Force One:* Scenes from this movie were shot at Cuyahoga County Courthouse and Severance Hall in Cleveland.

- *Captain America:* While this movie was set in Washington, D.C., it was actually filmed throughout Cleveland. The Cleveland Museum of Art, the West Shoreway, and downtown Cleveland are featured in the film.

- *Light of Day:* This 1987 movie featuring Michael J. Fox and Joan Jett about struggling musicians was filmed throughout Cleveland. The Euclid Tavern (which is now as the Happy Dog at Euclid Tavern today) is featured in the film.

- *Rain Man:* Some scenes from this movie were shot throughout Cincinnati. Some film locations include Children's Hospital Vernon Manor, the Dixie Terminal Building, and Columbia Parkway (U.S. Route 50).

- *Spider-Man 3:* Parts of the film were shot throughout downtown Cleveland, including Euclid Avenue.

- *The Avengers:* This superhero movie was shot throughout Cleveland, Cincinnati, Fairborn, Wilmington, and Parma, Ohio.

- *The Shawshank Redemption*: Scenes from the film, which is based on Stephen King's novel *Rita Hayworth and Shawshank Redemption*, were shot in Ohio. The scenes were filmed on location at the Ohio State Reformatory.

These are just a few of the many movies that were filmed in Ohio!

A '90s Boy Band Was Formed by Ohioans

Did you know that '90s boy band 98 Degrees was formed thanks to their ties to Ohio?

It all started out when Jeff Timmons, who was from Massillon, OH, made the decision to quit Kent State University in order to pursue a career in music. Timmons made the decision after he sang at a college party with a few friends and received a lot of positive feedback from females.

Timmons headed out to Los Angeles to pursue his music. It was there that he met a former student of the School for Creative and Performing Arts in Cincinnati. (Talk about a small world). The student put Timmons in touch with another former graduate of the school, who was attending Miami University in Oxford, Ohio at the time. That former graduate just so happened to be Nick Lachey, who would become the band's frontrunner.

Nick Lachey had another friend from the school who they invited to join the band: Justin Jeffre. Jeffre had been attending the University of Cincinnati at the time. The final member to join the band was Nick Lachey's younger brother Drew, who had been working as an EMT in New York City.

The rest is history! The band worked odd jobs while recording their first songs. At a time when other boy bands, such as NSYNC and the Backstreet Boys, had emerged, they set themselves apart by focusing on writing their own music and giving it an R&B/soul slant. Their first single, "Invisible Man," hit No. 12 on the *Billboard* Hot 100. They went on to record hit singles, "Because of You," "The Hardest Thing," "My Everything," and "I Do (Cherish You)."

This Cleveland Native Co-Produced A Show About a Fictionalized Version of Himself

If you're a fan of *The Drew Carey Show*, then you already know the show is set in Cleveland. What you might not know is that Drew Carey, the star of the series, is also a Cleveland native!

Carey grew up in Cleveland's Old Brooklyn neighborhood. He graduated from James Ford Rhodes High School, where he played the cornet and trumpet in the school's marching band. Carey later attended Kent State University where he was in a fraternity.

In the 1980s, Drew Carey got started in stand-up comedy. Carey won a contest at the Cleveland Comedy Club, which earned him the title of Master of Ceremonies. He made appearances on late night talk shows, including *The Tonight Show Starring Johnny Carson* and *Late Night with David Letterman.* He also began to earn small movie roles.

After working with Bruce Helford on the TV show *Someone Like Me*, the two went on to create and produce *The Drew Carey Show*. Carey has said that the fictionalized portrayal of himself is what he feels would have been his life if he hadn't gone into acting.

The Drew Carey Show ran from 1995 to 2004.

You might be disappointed to learn that while the show was set in Cleveland, most of it was filmed in Los Angeles.

The Author of *Goosebumps* is an Ohio Native

Did you know that R.L. Stine, author of the children's book series *Goosebumps*, is from Ohio?

Stine, whose real name is Robert Lawrence Stine, was born in Columbus, Ohio. He was raised in Bexley,

Ohio. It was there that he found his love of writing. When he was just nine years old, he found a typewriter in the attic of his home. He began to use the typewriter to write joke books and short stories.

R.L. Stine attended Ohio State University, where he earned a B.A. in English. During his time there, he was an editor for the college's humor magazine, *The Sundial.*

After Stine graduated from OSU in 1965, he moved to New York City in pursuit of his writing career. He first began his career under the pen name "Jovial Bob Stine." Under that name, he published numerous children's humor books and also created *Bananas*, a humor magazine that was published by Scholastic Press.

In 1986, he published his first horror book, *Blind Date,* under the pseudonym "R.L. Stine." He then went on to write other books, including *The Babysitter, Beach House, Hit and Run,* and *The Girlfriend.*

Stine also became the head writer and co-creator of the *Nickelodeon* show *Eureka's Castle*.

In the late 1980s, R.L. Stine began to publish his two most well-known book series: *Fear Street* and *Goosebumps*. He also wrote the *Mostly Ghostly, Rotten School,* and *Goosebumps Horrorland* series, along with a number of other novels.

R.L. Stine's books have even been made into several adaptations. Stine produced the *Goosebumps* TV show, as well as video games based on the series.

In 2015, *Goosebumps* made it to the big screen. Jack Black plays the fictionalized character of R.L. Stine. R.L. Stine also made an appearance in the movie!

And to think, it all started out with that typewriter in that attic of the house he grew up in Bexley, Ohio!

The World's Largest Drumsticks are in Ohio

Did you know the world's largest drumsticks can be found in Warren, Ohio?

They're located in an alley that's dedicated to drummer David Grohl, who was the former drummer for the band Nirvana and the founder of the band the Foo Fighters. Grohl was born in Warren, OH.

The alley, which opened in 2009, was created by Warren police sergeant Joe O'Grady. He thought the alleyway could help inspire Warren's youth. David Grohl attended the unveiling of the alleyway.

The alley is now known as David Grohl Alley. It contains a number of forms of artwork dedicated to David Grohl, including plywood canvasses and graffiti-style art depicting him.

O'Grady also wanted to add the "world's largest drumsticks" to help draw attraction to the alleyway.

The drumsticks, which were hand-carved by a local artist named Joel Eggert, measure 23 feet long and weigh half a ton!

Although David Grohl didn't attend the unveiling of the drumsticks when they were added to the alley back in 2013, it has been said that he can be seen roaming the alley on occasion. There have been numerous reports of tourists bumping into him when they stop by to check out the alley.

The "King of Cowboys" Was Born in the Queen City

Did you know one of the most famous Western actors of all time grew up in Ohio? Roy Rogers, who was known as the "King of Cowboys," was born in Cincinnati, AKA the Queen City.

Born as Leonard Slye, he and his family lived on 2nd Street where Riverfront Stadium was eventually built. Rogers often joked that he was born at second base. The family didn't live there long, however.

When Leonard was just a baby, his dad was unhappy with city life and built a houseboat. They used the boat to travel the Ohio River to Portsmouth, OH. They lived in the houseboat on land they purchased. They later purchased a farm near Lucasville, Ohio. His father worked at a shoe factory in Portsmouth during the week, living at home with the family on weekends.

He often brought home gifts for his children, including a horse that Len learned to ride on.

Since the family was forced to come up with their own entertainment, Len learned how to yodel and play the mandolin. He would square dance and sing with his family. Len and his mom often yodeled to communicate with one another on the farm.

Len went to high school in McDermott, Ohio until his sophomore year when his family moved back to Cincinnati. He quit school in order to help support the household. He worked at the same shoe factory as his father.

When his sister Mary moved to Lawndale, California, she suggested that Len audition for a radio program in Inglewood. He auditioned wearing a Western shirt that Mary had made for him. A few days later, Len was asked to join a country band called the Rocky Mountaineers.

In 1933, Len went on to form a country trio with Bob Nolan and Tim Spencer called the Pioneers Trio. A radio station announcer changed the band's name to Sons of the Pioneers since he felt they were too young to be called "pioneers." The band first grew popular in Los Angeles and then began to gain fame throughout the entire country.

The Sons of the Pioneers began to get movie roles, including their first full-length film, *The Old Homestead*.

When he was still known as Leonard Slye, he had a large supporting role as a cowboy alongside Gene Autry.

Slye became known as Roy Rogers after winning a competition for becoming a new singing cowboy after Autry began to demand more money for his work. Willie Phelps competed, but Slye ultimately won the competition.

"Roy Rogers" was chosen by shortening Leonard Slye's first name and combining it with Will Rogers' surname.

Under his new stage name, Roy Rogers, he was given the leading role in *Under Western Stars*. In many of his roles, Rogers played a character with his stage name.

Roy Rogers quickly rose to fame, competing with Gene Autry for America's favorite singing cowboy.

And to think the "King of Cowboys" was born in the Queen City!

Carmen Electra Was Classmates with This Singer

Did you know that Carmen Electra, whose real name is Tara Patrick, was born in Sharonville, Ohio? She attended the School for Creative and Performing Arts in Cincinnati. She played in a production of *Peter Pan* with a younger famous fellow classmate—Nick Lachey!

Patrick also went to Barbizon Modeling and Acting School in Cincinnati.

Her professional career started out at Kings Island amusement park in Mason, Ohio. She was a dancer in the park's show "It's Magic," which was one of the most popular productions put on by the park.

After she moved to Minneapolis, Tara Patrick met musician, Prince. She was given a recording contract with Prince's Paisley Park Records. It was through this brief music career that she became known as Carmen Electra.

In 1996, Electra was featured in *Playboy* magazine. This helped her earn a role in *Baywatch*. She also became well-known for her role as a host in the *MTV* show, *Singled Out*.

A Rat Pack Singer Got His Start in Ohio

Did you know Dean Martin was from Ohio? Born in Steubenville, his birth name was Dino Crocetti.

Growing up in Steubenville wasn't always the easiest for Crocetti. His first language was Italian, which was what his family spoke at home. Dino didn't speak English very well. When he attended Grant Elementary School in Steubenville, he was bullied because of his broken English.

When he was a teenager, Dino took up the drums as a hobby. He attended Steubenville High School, but he dropped out in the 10th grade because he thought he was smarter than his teachers. He went on to pursue numerous jobs, even pursuing boxing at 15 years old. He called himself "Kid Crochet" and ended up with a broken nose as a result of his fighting, which he later had straightened.

Eventually, he went on to sing with local bands. He began to call himself "Dino Martini," a name that was inspired by opera singer and actor Nino Martini. Dino Martini got his big break while he was working for the Ernie McKay Orchestra. By the late 1940s, he worked for the Sammy Watkins Band, which was based in Cleveland. Sammy Watkins suggested that he change his stage name to Dean Martin.

Dean Martin went on to meet Jerry Lewis at a comedy club in New York City, and the rest is history! A friendship was born and Dean Martin would go on to experience rat pack success.

A Famous Musician Got Her Name from a Bicycling Accident in Ohio

Macy Gray was born in Canton, Ohio. She bounced around to different schools, including one boarding school, before eventually graduating from Canton South High School. What some may not know about Macy Gray is that her real name is actually Natalie McIntyre.

When the singer was growing up in Ohio, she got into a bicycling accident. She noticed the name "Macy Gray" on someone's mailbox. The name stuck out to her. She used it when she wrote stories throughout her childhood. When her professional music career took off, the singer chose "Macy Gray" as her stage.

Gray, who is often called a "one-hit wonder," is most known for her '90s song "I Try."

"The Master of Horror" is From Ohio

It might surprise you to learn that Steven Spielberg isn't the only famous filmmaker who's from Ohio. The late Wes Craven was also a native of the Buckeye State. Wes Craven was born in Cleveland, Ohio.

Craven has been called "The Master of Horror" due to the cultural significance of his horror films.

Craven is most known for directing horror movies such as *A Nightmare on Elm Street*, *The Hills Have Eyes*, *The Last House on the Left*, *Scream*, *Scream 2*, and *Scream 3*.

It might surprise you to learn that, in spite of his nickname, Craven didn't always work—and didn't always want to work—in the horror genre. Craven started out his career as a pornographic film director. In 2005 documentary *Inside Deep Throat*, Craven admitted that he produced a lot of pornos under pseudonyms.

After the first film Craven directed, *The Last House on the Left*, was released in 1972, he received a lot of negative feedback. He hadn't been expecting the film to become as popular as it was. He tried to switch genres and wrote several non-horror films. They didn't receive any financial backers, however. The next film he received backing for was *The Hills Have Eyes*. At that point, Craven knew that his career would primarily be in the horror film genre (though he did later direct *Music of the Heart*).

There's no doubt that Wes Craven directed some of the best horror movies of all time—and it all started out in Cleveland!

RANDOM FACTS

1. Guy Fieri of *Diners, Drive-Ins, and Dives* fame was born in Columbus, Ohio.

2. Actress Sarah Jessica Parker is an Ohio native. The actress was born in Nelsonville and grew up in Cincinnati. Parker attended the School for Creative and Performing Arts in Cincinnati. Sarah Jessica Parker has said that while her family may have lived in Ohio, her mother always led what Parker calls a "New York lifestyle."

3. Former NSYNC member Chris Kirkpatrick went to Dalton High School in Dalton, Ohio.

4. A number of songs have been written about Ohio. One of the most famous is "Ohio is for Lovers" by Hawthorne Heights. Other songs written about Ohio include "Youngstown" by Bruce Springsteen, "Road Outside Columbus" by O.A.R., "My City Was Gone" by the Pretenders, "Cuyahoga" by R.E.M., and the official state song, "Beautiful Ohio" by Ballard MacDonald.

5. Singer/actress Doris Day was born in Cincinnati, Ohio.

6. Robert Burck, better known as "The Naked Cowboy," is from Cincinnati, Ohio. Today, he can

be found in his underwear in Times Square in New York City.

7. Mary Katherine Campbell, who was the 2nd woman in history to win Miss America and the only person in history to ever win the competition twice, was from Columbus, Ohio.

8. Actor Woody Harrelson was raised in Lebanon, Ohio. *The Hunger Games* star attended Lebanon High School and worked at Kings Island amusement park the summer he turned 18.

9. Actress Katie Holmes was born and raised in Toledo, Ohio. Holmes graduated from Notre Dame Academy in Toledo, an all-girls school. Katie Holmes performed in high school plays at St. John's Jesuit and St. Francis de Sales, all-boys schools in the area. She also took modeling classes in Toledo, which eventually led her to her first movie role in *The Ice Storm.*

10. A beloved actress from *The Golden Girls* starred in a show set in Cleveland. *Hot in Cleveland* features Betty White, along with Valerie Bertinelli, Jane Leeves, and Wendie Mallick. The series, which ran from 2010 to 2015, was *TV Land*'s highest telecast show in the network's history.

11. Marilyn Manson, whose real name is Brian Warner, was born and raised in Canton, Ohio, where he attended Heritage Christian School until

the 10th grade. He graduated from GlenOak High School in Plains Township in Ohio. He went to high school with Macy Gray at one point, but they never knew each other.

12. Late actor Paul Newman was born in Shaker Heights, OH. Some of his first performances were in his school's production of *Robin Hood* and the Cleveland Play House's *Saint George and the Dragon*. Today, Newman is most known for his roles in *The Hustler*, *Hud*, and *Butch Cassidy and the Sundance Kid*.

13. Actress Molly Shannon, who's most well-known for being a cast member on *Saturday Night Live*, was born in Shaker Heights, Ohio. The actress attended St. Dominic School in Shaker Heights, as well as Hawken School in Gates Mills, Ohio.

14. Rapper Bow Wow, formerly known as Lil' Bow Wow, was born in Columbus, Ohio. Born as Shad Moss, Bow Wow took an interest in rapping at the age of three. By the age of six, he was performing at concerts. He was noticed by Snoop Dogg at a concert in Los Angeles. Snoop Dogg chose his stage name "Lil' Bow Wow."

15. The Isley Brothers were from Cincinnati, Ohio. The trio of brothers—O'Kelly, Rudolph, and Ronald—were raised in the Lincoln Heights neighborhood before moving to Blue Ash, Ohio. They started out singing at their church.

16. American icon Annie Oakley was born in a log cabin near Woodland (today's Willowdell) in Ohio. She was a sharpshooter and exhibition shooter. Oakley's talent was recognized when she won a shooting match against Mark E. Butler, who she later went on to marry. Annie Oakley and Mark E. Butler joined *Buffalo Bill's Wild West* show, which led them to international fame. Oakley performed for a number of royals, including Queen Victoria of the United Kingdom.

17. Known for his roles in *Catch Me If You Can* and *Say Anything*, actor Martin Sheen was born in Dayton, Ohio. Sheen had a rough childhood. He suffered from polio as a child and lost his mother at 11.

18. Author and cartoonist James Thurber was born in Columbus, Ohio. He's best-known for his short story "The Secret Life of Walter Mitty," which has been adapted into two films.

19. The TV series *Glee* was set at William McKinley High School, a fictional Ohio high school. The town they show is set in—Lima, Ohio—is real, however.

20. After immigrating from London during his childhood, the late comedian/actor Bob Hope lived in Cleveland. Hope went to the Boys' Industrial School in Lancaster, OH, which he donated money to later in life.

Test Yourself – Questions and Answers

1. Which former '90s boy band member did _not_ live in Ohio at one point during his youth?

   a. Nick Lachey of 98 Degrees
   b. Justin Timberlake of NSYNC
   c. Chris Kirkpatrick of NSYNC

2. The Rock and Roll Hall of Fame is located in which city?

   a. Cleveland
   b. Columbus
   c. Cincinnati

3. Which superhero originated from two students in Cleveland?

   a. Batman
   b. Spider-Man
   c. Superman

4. You can visit the famous house from which movie in Cleveland?

   a. Home Alone
   b. A Christmas Story
   c. Elf

5. The author of which children's book series is from Columbus, Ohio?

   a. Harry Potter
   b. Goosebumps
   c. The Baby-Sitter's Club

Answers

1. b.

2. a.

3. c.

4. b.

5. b.

CHAPTER THREE

OHIO'S INVENTIONS, IDEAS, AND MORE!

Have you ever wondered what inventions come from the Buckeye State? It might surprise you to learn that a number of your favorite companies, restaurants, and products originated from Ohio. Do you know which famous fast food chain got its start in Ohio? Do you know which children's playtime product once started out as a cleaning product? Do you know what "Arby's" stands for? Hint: It's *not* "roast beef," contrary to whatever memes you may have seen floating around the internet. To find out what inventions you can thank the state of Ohio for, read on!

The First Gas-Powered Automobile

Did you know you can thank Ohio every time you start your car? While Karl Benz is credited with inventing the first car, the first practical gas-powered automobile was invented by an Ohio native.

John W. Lambert, of Ohio City, was the first person to invent a horseless buggy. Built in 1890, his invention had three wheels with a single cylinder, four-stroke engine. Today, his invention is known as the "Buckeye gasoline buggy."

Wendy's

Most known for its "old-fashioned" hamburgers and Frosty, Wendy's is the third largest fast food burger chain in the United States. Today there are more than 6,500 locations throughout the world, but did you know the first Wendy's opened in Columbus, Ohio back in 1969?

Founder Dave Thomas, who was from Kalamazoo, Michigan, was inspired to open a restaurant like Kewpee Hamburgers. Like Kewpee Hamburgers, the first Wendy's that Thomas opened in Columbus served malt shakes and square-shaped hamburgers that let customers see the quality of the meat.

The first franchisee opened a Wendy's in Indianapolis, Indiana in 1972. Today, more than 6,200 of Wendy's restaurants are owned by franchisees, while the company owns 330.

The first commercials for the restaurant, which were aired in Ohio, featured the slogan "Quality is Our Recipe."

The restaurant was named after Dave Thomas's daughter, Melinda Lou "Wendy" Thomas. The

Wendy's logo is based on Thomas's daughter when she was eight years old.

If you were hoping to visit the original Wendy's location in Columbus, you're out of luck. The restaurant shut down in 2007.

Today, Wendy's headquarters are based in Dublin, Ohio.

The Cash Register

Did you know the cash register was invented in Ohio?

A Dayton, Ohio native named James Ritty is credited with inventing the first cash register. The idea came about because Ritty, who owned a saloon back in 1871, had a lot of employees who stole money from his business.

When he was on a boat that was headed for Europe, Ritty drew inspiration from a machine that counted how many times the ship's propeller completed a rotation. He believed that he could create a machine that would track his sales using the same sort of technology.

Once he returned to Ohio, Ritty and his brother, a mechanic, designed the first cash register. When he had the invention patented in 1879, he named it "Ritty's Incorruptible Cashier."

One difference between Ritty's invention and the cash

registers of today? His cash register didn't have a drawer. It just worked to track sales and money.

Once his cash register had been patented, Ritty founded a company in Dayton to manufacture his product. However, there wasn't much interest among business owners and Ritty was forced to shut down his company. He sold his patent to an Ohio investor named John H. Patterson, who went on to turn the investment into a big business.

Ritty stayed in the saloon business after the sale.

Kroger

Today, there are more than 2,700 Kroger supermarkets and it's the 3rd largest supermarket in the world! Did you know that the supermarket chain started out in Ohio?

It all started out back in 1883 when Bernard "Barney" Kroger used his life savings of $372 (or the 2018 equivalent of $9,800) to open a grocery store in downtown Cincinnati.

Kroger had a motto that he followed when running his store: "Be particular. Never sell anything you would not want yourself."

This motto seemed to serve him well. By the following year, Kroger had opened a second location. The chain continued to grow.

Bernard Kroger made some innovating changing to his grocery stores, paving the way to modern grocery stores as we know them. Before Kroger, grocery stores purchased their bread from bakeries. Kroger was the first to realize that by baking his own bread, he could reduce retail prices on baked goods and still earn money.

Not only was Kroger the first supermarket to include bakeries in their stores, but they were also the first to sell both groceries *and* meats/seafood.

Play-Doh

In 2003, Play-Doh made the Toy Industry Association's "Century of Toys List." It may have even been one of your own favorite childhood pastimes. Did you know you can thank the Buckeye State for the invention?

It might surprise you to learn that Play-Doh was not originally designed for children to play with!

Play-Doh was first developed by Noah McVicker and his family-owned soap manufacturing company Kutol Products, which was based in Cincinnati. McVicker developed the putty when Kroger Grocery was in search of a product that would clean coal residue from wallpaper. The concoction of flour, water, salt, boric acid, and mineral oil worked like a charm.

In the 1950s, people began to switch from coal heat to natural gas. This meant there was less of a demand for the wallpaper cleaner. As sales of the product began to decrease, an idea came about to save Kutol Products from bankruptcy.

Noah McVicker's nephew, Joe McVicker, learned that children in schools were using the putty for art projects. They knew they need to give the putty a new name, so they designed on Play-Doh and began a new company under the name Rainbow Crafts Company to manufacture it.

When it was released in 1956, Play-Doh was an instant success. It was sold by department stores, like Macy's in New York City and Marshall Field's in Chicago. The product was advertised on kids shows like *Captain Kangaroo*.

Play-Doh sales reached $3 million during its first year!

To date, more than 700 million pounds of Play-Doh have been sold worldwide.

Chewing Gum

Did you know an Ohio native is the first to ever get a patent for chewing gum?

Dentist William Finley Semple designed gum to help clean the teeth and strengthen the jaw muscles.

However, Semple's chewing gum was very different from the gum we chew today. It wasn't sweet (or minty) in flavor. The ingredients in Semple's gum included rubber, chalk, powdered licorice root, and even charcoal in some variations.

Semple filed a patent for his invention in December of 1869.

Although most historians credit Semple as the first to have a chewing gum patent, Amos Tyler of Toledo, Ohio patented his own chewing gum in July of 1869—prior to Semple's patent. Tyler's recipe for chewing gum was quite different from Semple's, however. His was made from white rosin and olive oil.

Despite being the first to patent chewing gum, neither Ohio native was the first to actually invent it. The first documented seller of chewing gum was Maine native John B. Curtis, who sold "State of Main Pure Spruce Gum" back in 1848, for which he never received a patent.

Life Savers Candy

Today, most Americans are familiar with Life Savers candies, which are round candies with a hole in the center that come in a paper-wrapped, aluminum-foil roll. Did you know Life Savers have been around since the 1900s or that they were invented in the Buckeye State?

They were first created back in 1912 by Clarence Crane. Crane was a candy maker based in Cleveland, Ohio. He wanted to invent a candy that wouldn't melt

in his children's hands like chocolate did in summer —
and he did.

He created a line of hard mints, but he didn't have any
means of producing them since he lacked space and
machinery. Crane contracted a pill manufacturing
company, who pressed the mints into shape.

Crane ended up selling the formula for his Life Savers
to Edward Noble of New York in 1913. It was Noble
who began to package the mints into tin foil rolls — a
process that was done by hand until machinery
eventually became available.

Quaker Oatmeal

Did you know oatmeal was invented in Ohio?

German immigrant Ferdinand Schumacher owned a
small grocery store in Akron, Ohio in 1851. He sold
oats in his store, but he had a hard time selling it.
While people in Akron bought oats as livestock feed,
they didn't want to buy it for themselves. This led
Schumacher to experiment with new ways to package
his oats.

In 1854, Schumacher designed machinery that
chopped oats into small cubes that he sold in glass
jars. In 1856, there was such a demand for his cubed
oats that he bought an old factory that allowed him to
produce 20 barrels of oats a day. This was the start of
Schumacher's German Mills American Oatmeal
Company.

It was Schumacher who found a way to make cooking oats quicker. He precooked oats and turned them into flakes before they were sold.

The American Civil War drove business, with the Union Army buying Schumacher's oats to feed soldiers. By 1863, business was hopping and Schumacher bought a mill on Mill Street in Akron, which is today known as "Quaker Square."

Schumacher began to be recognized as "The Oatmeal King."

In 1901, Schumacher merged his German Mills American Oatmeal Company with the Quaker Mill Company, which was based in Ravenna, Ohio and owned by Henry Parsons Crowell. Crowell had been selling his Quaker Oats in packages with preparation directions on the back. The two companies also merged with a large cereal mill in Cedar Rapids, Iowa. The merger of these three companies formed Quaker Oats Company!

Buffalo Wild Wings

Did you know restaurant/bar chain Buffalo Wild Wings started out in the Buckeye State?

Originally called Buffalo Wild Wings & Weck, the first location was established by Jim Disbrow and Scott Lowery in 1982.

The idea came about when Disbrow and Lowery met

after Disbrow judged a figuring skating competition at Kent State University. They wanted to get Buffalo-style chicken wings, but they couldn't find any restaurant in the surrounding area that served them.

Disbrow and Lowery opened their first location near Ohio State University, Columbus. They chose the name "Buffalo Wild Wings & Weck" because the menu included both buffalo wings and beef on weck.

Over the course of the next 10 years, Buffalo Wild Wings began to expand to six more locations throughout Ohio, Indiana, and Colorado.

In 1992, they began to franchise.

Today, there are more than 1,230 Buffalo Wild Wings throughout the United States.

Arby's

Did you know that the fast food chain Arby's started out in Ohio?

Co-founders, brothers Forrest and Leroy Raffel, saw the market potential of a fast food business that wasn't based on hamburgers. They originally wanted to call the chain "Big Tex," but it was already used by another business located in Akron. They chose the name "Arby's," due to the pronunciation of "R.B." — after the Raffel Brothers.

In July of 1964, the Raffel brothers opened their first

Arby's location in Boardman, Ohio. The first menu items only included roast beef sandwiches, potato chips, and soft drinks. They tried to target a more upscale customer base, so they sold their sandwiches for $0.69 while hamburgers were generally $0.15 at the time.

The model worked. By the 1970s, Arby's began to grow at a rate of 50 stores each year. The chain also began to add more menu items, such as its famous Jamocha Shakes, the Beef 'n Cheddar, and chicken sandwiches. They also introduced their signature sauces: Arby's Sauce and Horsey Sauce. In 1988, they introduced their famous Curly-Q Fries (Curly Fries).

In 1991, Arby's was the first fast-food chain to offer a "lite" menu with salads and sandwiches under 300 calories.

Today, there are more than 3,300 Arby's locations throughout the world. The fast-food chain ranks 3rd in terms of revenue.

The Portable Electric Vacuum Cleaner

Love vacuuming or hate it, it's hard to imagine a world without vacuum cleaners. Did you know the first portable electric vacuum cleaner was invented by a department store janitor in Canton, Ohio?

Back in 1907, janitor James Murray Spangler designed the product. His invention was unique in a couple of ways. It had a suction that, with the help of an electric fan, blew the dirt and dust into a separate container (which he had constructed from a soapbox and a pillowcase). Additionally, his invention had a rotating brush that loosened debris.

Unfortunately, Spangler wasn't able to produce his invention because of lack of funding. He sold the patent to William Henry Hoover, who manufactured leather goods in the Canton area. Hoover made several changes to Spangler's design, including casters, attachments, and steel casing.

In 1922, the Hoover Company was formed. The first Hoover vacuum model sold for $60. Over the years, the company added new technologies, including "the beater bar," disposable filter bags, and an upright vacuum cleaner.

Dum Dums Lollipops

Did you know Dum Dums lollipops originated from Ohio?

They were invented at Akron Candy Company in Bellevue, Ohio back in 1924. I.C. Bahr, who was a manager at the company, gave them the name "Dum Dums" with the idea that any child would be able to say it.

The Spangler Candy Company purchased Dum Dums in 1953. They began manufacturing them in Bryan, Ohio.

The first Dum Dums only came in seven flavors. They were butterscotch, cherry, lemon, lime, coconut-pineapple, grape, and orange. Today, Dum Dums come in 16 flavors!

Stouffer's

Stouffer's frozen meals are a convenience that many of us take for granted. If you're wondering who you can thank for them, it's Abraham E. Stouffer and his father who started the family business back in Medina County, Ohio in 1914.

It might surprise you to learn that Stouffer's didn't start out selling frozen foods right away.

In 1914, the Stouffer family opened the Medina County Creamery and a dairy stand at Sheriff Street Market in Cleveland.

In 1922, Abraham and his wife Lena converted one of their dairy stands into a restaurant. Located at the Cleveland Arcade, they sold sandwiches, buttermilk, and Lena's homemade Dutch apple pie. The apple pie was a hit, leading the restaurant to immediate success. At one point, it was one of the top-rated restaurants in the city.

They later opened a second restaurant on East Ninth Street in Cleveland. This restaurant was called Stouffer Lunch.

The Stouffer family continued to expand their business.

In 1929, the Stouffer's opened locations outside of Ohio. They opened a restaurant in Detroit, Michigan and another in Pittsburgh, Pennsylvania.

In 1936, Abraham died. His two sons continued the business. They continued with their expansions, opening a restaurant in New York City and even buying hotels.

In 1946—ten years after Abraham's death—Stouffer's entered the frozen food market. That's where the company gained most of its success.

Today, Stouffer's is well-known for its frozen lasagna, macaroni and cheese, and Salisbury steak and its Lean Cuisine line of frozen meals.

Although some former Stouffer's restaurants remain open today as Select restaurants, the company is primarily focused on its frozen entrees.

Big Lots

Today, there are more than 1,400 Big Lots stores in 47 states. Did you know the chain originated in Ohio—and that there was early controversy over the store's name?

In 1967, Consolidated Stores Corporation was formed by Sol Shenk. The corporation opened its first closeout store, Odd Lots, in Columbus, OH in 1967.

In 1983, Revco, a drugstore chain, bought out closeout retailer Odd Lot Trading Co. At the same time,

Consolidated Stores Corporation continued to expand its Odd Lot stores throughout Columbus. Revco was unhappy that there was a company using a similar name and a similar business model.

Consolidated Stores Corporation and Revco reached an agreement. Consolidated Stores Corp. would only use the name Odd Lots within a certain mile radius of Columbus. Outside of that radius, Consolidated Stores Corp.'s stores would be called "Big Lots."

Over time, all of Consolidated Stores Corporation's stores were renamed to Big Lots.

Buckeye Candy

Ohio State Buckeye Candy, which is often called "Buckeye Candy" for short, is one of Ohio's little treasures you won't want to miss out on.

This candy is similar to peanut butter balls. The balls are made from peanut butter, butter, and powdered sugar. Vanilla extract may be included in some recipes. Once the balls are formed, they're refrigerated for about an hour. The balls are then dipped in melted chocolate.

The balls are called "Ohio State Buckeyes" because they resemble buckeye nuts. When dipping the candy, a small part of the peanut butter ball is left undipped to give it the appearance of a buckeye nut.

Buckeye Candy is a popular homemade treat, but you

can also find Buckeye Candy through candy catalogs or at candy shops throughout the state. It's also popular in Ohio's neighboring states.

RANDOM FACTS

1. Bob Evans Restaurants started out in Ohio. Founded by Bob Evans, the chain started out when he began packaging and processing sausage at his farm in Rio Grande, Ohio. Once it grew in popularity, he began to serve it at his diner in Gallipolis, OH—and Bob Evans Restaurants was born!

2. Skyline Chili is a favorite among Cincinnatians. The chain restaurant serves its famous chili, a secret recipe that the chain allegedly keeps in a bank vault! Its most popular menu items are chili and cheese served on spaghetti and "cheese coneys" (hot dogs with chili, cheese, onions, and mustard). Skyline's canned chili sauce can also be found in grocery stores.

3. Steubenville-style pizza originated from—you guessed it—Steubenville, Ohio! Unlike other styles of pizza, the cheese is added to the pie *after* it comes out of the oven. This is done to help preserve the flavor of the cheese.

4. United Dairy Farmers started out in Norwood, Ohio. The ice cream/frozen yogurt, coffee, and gasoline chain was started by Carl Lindner and

children. Lindner thought opening the store could help cut out the milkmen, which would save money for consumers. Today, UDF stores can be found throughout the Greater Cincinnati area, Dayton, and Columbus, OH.

5. Arc lamp street lights were invented by Euclid, Ohio native Charles Brush, who first tested them out in Cleveland's Public Square. Meaning Downtown Cleveland was the first city to *ever* be lit by street lamps.

6. The first electric rail streetcar was also designed by Charles Brush. This invention was also introduced in Cleveland.

7. The first gas mask was invented by Garrett Morgan of Cleveland. It was known as a "smoke hood." His invention saved the lives of both firefighters and miners. The gas mask used in World War I was also based on his invention.

8. A curved-tooth comb and a hair straightening liquid were also some of Garett Morgan's inventions.

9. Thomas Edison was born in Milan, Ohio, so we can *technically* thank the Buckeye State for some of his inventions—which include the light bulb and the phonograph!

10. Sherwin-Williams Stores were founded by Henry

Sherwin and Edward Williams back in 1866. The first store opened in Cleveland.

11. Bath and Body Works started out in New Albany, Ohio in 1990. By 1997, it had become the leading bath and fragrance chain shop in America.

12. Stanley Steemer started out in Dublin, Ohio in 1947. Since then, it's been the most popular carpet cleaning business. Today, there are more than 300 Stanley Steemer locations throughout 48 states.

13. The first indoor shopping complex in the United States was located in Ohio. It was the Cleveland Arcade. Opened in 1890, it was known for its iconic skylight.

14. Dayton C. Miller, a physicist at the Case School of Applied Science at Cleveland's Case Western University, invented the first full-body scanning technology of its kind. This technology has helped pave the way for MRIs and CAT scans done today.

15. The first semi truck in the entire world was invented in Cleveland by Alexander Winton in 1898!

16. Teflon was discovered by chemistry Roy J. Plunkett. The Ohio native invented it on accident. He realized that the white powder left over from a refrigeration gas experiment he performed at

DuPont was heat resistant, despite being as slippery as ice.

17. The pop top can, like those used for soda cans, was invented in Dayton, Ohio. It was designed by Ermal Cleon Fraze. Like the pop top cans of today, there was a ring attached to the rivet that could be pulled and then later discarded.

18. The zipper wasn't invented in Ohio, but it *did* get its name in the state. Akron-based B.F. Goodrich came up with the name in 1923, due to the sound they make. Goodrich called their galoshes Zipper Boots. In the late 1920s, the University of Akron had a contest to name its athletics teams and the "Zippers" won. The university's mascot is named "Zippy."

19. Artificial fish bait was designed by Ohio-based Pfleuger Fishing Tackle.

20. Iams Pet Food started out in Ohio. It was designed by Paul Iams, who was an animal nutritionist. He originally established the company in a feed mill near Dayton, OH. Iams created the world's first animal-based protein, dry dog food. Paul Iams also created Eukanuba dog food.

Test Yourself – Questions and Answers

1. Which fast food chain did *not* start out in Ohio?

    a. Arby's
    b. Wendy's
    c. Burger King

2. Which supermarket chain started out in Ohio?

    a. Publix
    b. Kroger
    c. Food Lion

3. Ferdinand Schumacher was known as:

    a. The Candy King
    b. The Oatmeal King
    c. The Vacuum King

4. Steubenville-style pizza is unique because:

    a. The cheese is added after the pizza's cooked
    b. The cheese goes on before the sauce
    c. There isn't cheese on the pizza

5. Dum Dums lollipops were first invented by:

    a. The Akron Candy Company
    b. The Spangler Candy Company
    c. Stouffer's

Answers

1. c.
2. b.
3. b.
4. a.
5. a.

CHAPTER FOUR

FACTS ABOUT OHIO'S ATTRACTIONS

Have you ever wondered what there is to see and do in Ohio? From amusement parks to a national park, there are so many things to check out in the Buckeye State. But how much do you really know about the state's attractions? Do you know which amusement park ride was once featured in an episode of one of America's favorite sitcoms? Do you know which American hero's body can be found in the state? Hint: it's not a human! Do you know which odd museums can be found in the state? To find out the answers to these questions and to learn more about Ohio's attractions, read on!

The "Roller Coaster Capital of the World" is Located in Ohio

Did you know Ohio is home to the "Roller Coaster Capital of the World"?

Cedar Point, an amusement park located near Sandusky, Ohio and Lake Erie, is one of the most popular tourist destinations in the Buckeye State. The park boasts itself as the "Roller Coaster Capital of the World." With 18 roller coasters, Cedar Point is the park with the 2nd highest number of roller coasters in the United States as of 2018. (Six Flags Magic Mountain in Valencia, California ranks at No. 1 with 19 roller coasters).

With more than 10 miles (or 50,727 feet) of roller coaster track, Cedar Point has a lot of rides to offer. Children will enjoy the Woodstock Express or Wilderness Run. More seasoned thrill seekers will want to try out Cedar Point's famous Top Thrill Dragster, which will take you 420 feet in the air at a whopping 120 mph in 17 seconds!

In 2018, Cedar Point unveiled its newest roller coaster addition: Steel Vengeance. It's the tallest, fastest, and longest steel-on-wood hybrid roller coaster in the entire world. The coaster stands 205 feet tall and drops you 200 feet at 74 mph. Talk about an adventure.

If you're not into roller coasters, that's okay. Cedar Point has a number of other attractions that might be of interest. There are a number of other thrill rides, family rides, and Cedar Point Shores Water Park. The park is also well-known for its three unique carousels, which offer more than 160 animals you can ride on.

Cedar Point is the 2nd oldest amusement park in the United States. The park first opened in 1870. At that time, it was a beer garden, dancehall, and bathhouse. The park's first roller coaster, the Switchback Railway, didn't open until 1892.

Cedar Point is the No. 1 most visited amusement park in the U.S. In 2017, the park saw 3.6 million visitors.

Kings Island Amusement Park Also Holds Some Impressive Roller Coaster Records

While it may not boast itself as the "Roller Coaster Capital of the World" the way Cedar Point does, Kings Island amusement park *does* hold some pretty impressive records in terms of roller coasters.

When Kings Island amusement park opened in Mason, OH back in 1972, the popularity of roller coasters was dwindling. But in 1973, the show *The Brady Bunch* featured the Racer, one of Kings Island's wooden roller coasters. It's believed that this revived the country's interest in roller coasters. The Racer is still located at the park today.

The park's roller coaster the Beast is the tallest, fastest, and longest wooden roller coaster in the entire world. Therefore, it's not surprising that the Beast consistently remains one of the world's top coasters, making it the top 10 list in *Amusement Today*. Since it was unveiled in 1979, the ride has been ridden over 53 million times and remains one of the park's top attractions.

The Banshee is another roller coaster that sets a record. Thanks to its 4,124 feet tracks, the Banshee is the longest inverted roller coaster in the world. When the ride opened back in 2014, it was also the first inverted roller coaster that had been built since 2006.

If you're not into roller coasters, Kings Island has plenty of other great attractions to offer. There's everything from kid-friendly rides at Planet Snoopy and an animal safari at Action Zone to a water park at Soak City!

Kings Island is the second most visited tourist attraction in the state (passed up only by Cedar Point, of course).

Columbus Zoo Was Once Home to Colo the Gorilla

You may have heard about Colo the Gorilla, but what to do you really know about this magnificent animal?

Born at Columbus Zoo and Aquarium, Colo was the first gorilla to have ever been bred in captivity. At the time of her death, she was also the oldest captive gorilla in the entire world. Her parents, Millie and Mac, arrived in Columbus back in 1951 after being caught in the wild in the French Cameroon.

Colo got her name from *Colu*mbus, *Ohio*. Before this

name was officially chosen, she was originally named Cuddles.

When Colo died at 60 years of age in 2017, she had not only outlived her estimated life expectancy by 20 years and held the record for gorilla longevity. During her time at the Columbus Zoo, where she was born and died, Colo gave experts a vast amount of knowledge about her species.

Colo also contributed to the Columbus Zoo's gorilla conservation efforts. At the time of her death, she had three children, 16 grandchildren, 12 great-grandchildren, and three great-great-grandchildren.

While Colo is no longer at the zoo, there are other gorillas to see. There Columbus Zoo and Aquarium is home to over 10,000 animals. While visiting the zoo, you can check out Asia Quest, Congo Expedition, Heart of Africa, Shores and Aquarium, and more.

One of the zoo's biggest attractions in winter is Wildlights, a holiday celebration in the zoo which features over three million lights.

In the summertime, there's also Zoombezi Bay Waterpark.

Ohio is Home to One of the Largest State Fairs

Did you know the Buckeye State is home to one of the largest state fairs in the USA?

The Ohio State Fair, which is held in Columbus, OH each year, is one of the most visited fairs in the country. The fair generally sees more than 800,000 visitors a year. In 2015, the Ohio State Fair had 982,305 visitors—the highest number of visitors the fair has ever seen.

It's no surprise that the fair is one of the most visited. It has some pretty cool attractions, including camel rides, pig races, and a petting zoo. Major musicians and artists perform at the fair each year. The "Buckeye Health Plan SkyGlider" is one of the longest portable sky rides *in the entire world!*

The first Ohio State Fair was held in 1850. The state has held a fair every year since then, except for 1942-1945 due to World War II.

It's been estimated that roughly $68.5 million dollars that's earned from the fair contribution to the Ohio state economy each year.

You Might Reconsider Fishing in the Cuyahoga Valley National Park

If you're thinking about visiting Cuyahoga Valley National Park, you might be thinking about going fishing while you're there. Well, think again.

You might remember from the first chapter that the Cuyahoga River was one of the most polluted rivers in the country at one point, causing it to catch on fire at least 13 times. In 1969, the river was cleaned up. However, it's still not recommended for parkgoers to fish in the river. Although you *can* fish while you're there, catch-and-release is strongly encouraged. People are not advised to eat the fish they catch at the river.

There are plenty of other things to do and see at the park. You can hike across 125 miles of trails or go bird and nature watching. You'll find 194 species of birds in the park. You might also see gray and red foxes, white-tailed deer, beavers, coyotes, and other animals. You can stay at one of the five campsites that can be found throughout the park. You might also check out some of Cuyahoga Valley National Park's biggest attractions, such as Brandywine Falls and the Beaver Marsh.

Cuyahoga Valley National Park, which is considered to be one of the most accessible national parks in the country, spans across 33,000 acres of land. The park sees approximately two million visitors per year!

You Can Take a Train Ride Through Cuyahoga Valley National Park

Did you know you can take a train excursion through Cuyahoga Valley National Park?

The Cuyahoga Valley Scenic Railroad offers trips through Peninsula, Ohio. The primary focus on the trip is generally Cuyahoga Valley National Park. Although you can take train excursions through the area at any time, autumn is a popular time to see scenic views in the region. Tours can be taken from Independence to Akron, Ohio.

During the months of November and December, the Cuyahoga Valley Scenic Railroad also runs the Polar Express. The holiday-themed ride is based on the book/movie of the same name.

Cleveland Metroparks is Larger Than Central Park

Did you know Cleveland Metroparks is larger than Central Park in New York City? While NYC spans across 843 acres, Cleveland Metroparks encompasses 23,000 acres of land!

Made up of 18 reservations, you'll find more than 300 miles of trails, eight lakefront parks, eight golf courses, and the Cleveland Metroparks Zoo, which is home to a simulated rainforest!

Cleveland Metroparks is made up of the following reservations:

- Acacia Reservation
- Bedford Reservation
- Big Creek Reservation
- Bradley Woods Reservation

- Brecksville Reservation,
- Brookside Reservation
- Euclid Creek Reservation
- Garfield Park Reservation
- Hinckley Reservation
- Huntington Reservation
- Lakefront Reservation
- Mill Stream Run Reservation
- North Chagrin Reservation
- Ohio & Erie Canal Reservation
- Rocky River Reservation
- South Chagrin Reservation
- Washington Reservation
- West Creek Reservation

One of the Most Popular Art Museums in the World is in Ohio

Did you know that one of the most visited art museums *in the entire world* can be found right in Cleveland, Ohio?

The Cleveland Museum of Art sees an average of more than 700,000 visitors each year. And it's no surprise, either. The museum has so much to offer with its 45,000 pieces of artwork. Its collections include pieces from Monet, Vincent Van Gogh, Picasso, and other famous artists.

The museum is best known for its Asian and Egyptian art collections. Its Asian collection of artwork has been said to be the best in America. The museum is also popular for its collection of medieval artwork, including armor.

The museum is also home to a bronze sculpture of *Apollo*, which is thought to be an original masterpiece of Praxiteles of Athens of the 4th century BC.

You Can Visit the Official Museum of the U.S. Airforce

If you're a military or history buff, then you may already know the official museum is located near Dayton, Ohio.

The National Museum of the United States Airforce is one of the most visited attractions in Ohio. The museum draws in approximately one million guests each year.

A lot of the museum is devoted to the Wright brothers. There are a number of artifacts involving the brothers, including a replica of the 1909 Military Flyer. The museum is also located at Wright-Patterson Air Force Base, which was named, in part, after the famous aviation brothers.

Today, the museum is home to over 360 aircraft and missiles, making it the largest collection in the world. Most of the aircraft on display at the museum are rare or are technologically significant, such as the Boeing B-29 Superfortress or "Bockscar" (which dropped an atomic bomb on Nagasaki during World War II), the North American XB-70 Valkyrie, and the only four Convair B-36 Peacemakers that are still in existence today.

The museum's Presidential Gallery has several aircraft on display that was used by former American presidents. Some of those include Franklin D. Roosevelt, Harry Truman, Dwight D. Eisenhower, John F. Kennedy, Lyndon B. Johnson, and Richard Nixon. The aircraft that transported President John F. Kennedy and his wife to Dallas, Texas on the day of his assassination is also on display at the museum.

Ohio is Home to the Second Oldest Zoo in the USA—And It's Where One of the World's Biggest Tragedies Has Happened

Did you know the second oldest zoo can be found in the Buckeye State?

The Cincinnati Zoo and Botanical Garden, which opened in 1875, is the second oldest zoo in the country. (The first oldest is the Philadelphia Zoo, which opened the year before).

In 2014, the Cincinnati Zoo was ranked as one of the top zoos in the country by *USA Today*.

Since the zoo opened in 1875, it has made a few records. Some of these records include:

- The longest living alligator in captivity (which lived to 70 years of age)
- The fastest cheetah living in captivity
- It was once home to the largest Komodo dragon living in captivity

The Cincinnati Zoo is also one of the only zoos in North America to ever have a Bonobo breeding program.

The zoo received a lot of attention back in May of 2016 when a three-year-old boy climbed into the enclosure of a Western lowland gorilla named Harambe. The incident went viral when a zoogoer got video footage of the incident and uploaded it to YouTube. The video showed that Harambe dragged the child around, even hitting his head on concrete. Zoo officials were forced to kill Harambe in order to save the boy, sparking nationwide controversy.

You Can Visit President McKinley's Burial Spot

Located in Canton, Ohio, the William McKinley Presidential Library and Museum honors the former U.S. President's life.

The museum is dedicated to preserving the life of the former assassinated president. You'll learn more about McKinley's life. The facility is home to numerous artifacts, including William McKinley's piano, rocking chair, home furnishings, and more.

You'll also find the William McKinley Memorial, where the president was laid to rest. The memorial, which is covered by a dome, is open for guests to visit between the months of April and November.

While this might seem like an unusual place for a body to be buried, quite the contrary. Canton was McKinley's home, so it makes perfect sense that it would be his final resting spot.

The Sixth Largest Open Historic Home is in Ohio

Did you know the 6th largest historic home that's open to the public can be found in Ohio? It's called Stan Hywet Hall & Gardens and it's located in Akron.

The home was built by F.A. Seiberling, who founded the Goodyear Tire and Rubber Company. The name "Stan Hywet" originated from Old English and means "stone quarry."

There are original furnishings that can be found in the manor, and you'll also get to take a tour of the 70 acres of grounds and gardens. The English Garden is of particular interest to many, as it was designed by famous landscaper, Ellen Biddle Shipman, during the late 1920s.

Toledo Museum of Art is Every Glass Art Lover's Dream

The Toledo Museum of Art is home to more than 30,000 pieces of artwork, which include everything from ancient Greek and Roman to contemporary and modern. But there's one thing that sets the Toledo Museum of Art apart from any other: its glass art.

It's no surprise that the Toledo Museum of Art is well-known for its glass artwork since the museum was actually founded by glassmaker Edward Drummond Libbey in 1901.

Not only is the museum home to a large collection of glass art, but it's also known for its Glass Pavilion, which opened in 2006.

The Glass Pavilion, which was designed by Frank Gehry, has a unique design. It's made from glass wall both on the interior and exterior. It has received a lot of praise.

The pavilion also houses the museum's glass artwork collection. Both the original pieces and new works, including one of Dale Chihuly's sculptures, can be found in the building.

There's a Castle You Can Visit in the Buckeye State

Ohio might not seem like a place where you'd visit a castle, but you can!

Located in Loveland, Ohio, the castle was built by bachelor Harry Andrews. He was 55 years old when started building the castle, a smaller-scale version of a Medieval castle. Andrews was a Medieval enthusiast.

Constructing the castle entirely on his own, a lot of work went into the project. Andrews built the castle from 56,000 pails of stone and more than 2,500 sacks of cement.

What became of Harry Andrews? He, tragically, set himself on fire in the castle. He died two weeks after the incident. Today, "Knights of the Golden Trail"—a youth organization that Andrews founded before his death—run the castle.

It may (or may not) surprise you to learn that the castle is believed to be haunted by Harry Andrews himself.

An American (Canine) Hero's Body Can Be Found at an Ohio Museum

You've probably heard of Balto, the heroic sled dog who led a team to deliver medicine from Anchorage to Nome, Alaska, in spite of brutal winds and below freezing temperatures. The medicine helped save Nome residents during a bad outbreak of diphtheria in 1925.

Balto is widely regarded as an America hero. A film called *Balto* was based on his journey. There's even a statue in the sled dog's honor at Central Park in New York City.

But did you know Balto's body, which is preserved through taxidermy, can be found in Ohio?

You might be wondering how an Alaskan sled dog's body ended up all the way in Ohio. The story is actually pretty tragic.

Because of the attention Balto had drawn, owner Gunner Kaassen decided to use him and the rest of the sled dog team to make money. The team ended up in a dime museum in Los Angeles where they were said to be in poor condition.

But Balto and the rest of Kaassen's sled dog team still managed to get their happy ending.

George Kimble, a businessman from Cleveland, found the dogs on a trip to the museum. Shocked by what poor condition they were in, Kimble started a campaign to raise the $2,000 Kaassen wanted to sell them for. Fortunately, he was able to raise the money.

In 1927, Balto and the other sled dogs were brought to Cleveland. They lived out the rest of their lives at the Cleveland Metroparks Zoo.

In 1933, Balto died at 14 years old. His body was preserved through taxidermy. It was taken to the Cleveland Museum of Natural History, which is where you'll find it today.

Some of the other attractions you'll find at the Cleveland Museum of Natural History include the only small tyrannosaur *Nanotyrannus lancensis* in existence today, mastodon and mammoth specimens, the Fannye Shafran Planetarium, the Jeptha Wade gem collection, a moon rock, and more.

RANDOM FACTS

1. Coney Island in Cincinnati (which has *no* connection to Coney Island in Long Island, New York) opened in 1886. It started out as an apple orchard on the banks of the Ohio River. Today, it's a small amusement park and waterpark.

2. Lucky Cat Museum, which is located in Cincinnati, is home to more than 1,000 artifacts of the Lucky Cat. The Lucky Cat, or Maneki-neko, is a symbol from Japan that dates back more than a century!

3. The Toledo Zoo has helped in conserving the monarch butterfly, the Aruba Island rattlesnake, the West Indian boa, and the Kihansi spray toad (which they were able to restore after it had previously been declared extinct). Many of the zoo's conservation efforts are done abroad!

4. Cincinnati's Fountain Square is a popular meeting spot in the city. In winter, there's an ice skating rink. There are restaurants, coffee shops, and music and entertainment that you can enjoy at any time of year. The Tyler Davidson Fountain was dedicated to the square back in 1871.

5. Hocking Hills State Park is one of the most

popular state parks in Ohio. Located in Hocking County, the park draws in over 2.9 million visitors on a yearly basis.

6. There are a number of wineries located along Lake Erie and in the surrounding area. The state's winemaking history started out in the 1850s, and wineries continue to remain a popular attraction today.

7. The Akron Zoo is home to more than 700 species of animals. The zoo is most well-known for its grizzly bear exhibit.

8. Portage Lakes State Park is situated on 2,034 acres of land. It's located in New Franklin, Ohio.

9. Crystal Cave in Put-In-Bay, Ohio is the largest geode in the world. When you enter the limestone "cave", you're actually entering a single rock.

10. Mohican State Park, which is located in Ashland County, OH, is a popular place for people who enjoy camping, hiking, biking, fishing, and other outdoor activities.

11. The National First Ladies' Library in Canton, Ohio is dedicated to the preservation and education of the former USA's First Ladies. The facility is located in the restored McKinley house. You'll learn more about flirting throughout history, the former First Ladies' relationships and ancestry, and see mini replicas of their gowns.

12. The Canton Classic Car Museum was founded by Marshall Beldon, Sr. back in 1978. The museum is home to the Holmes automobile, which was built right in Canton, Ohio. It's just one of the many rare and antique cars that can be found at the museum.

13. The "Frozen Cleveland Lighthouse" is a lighthouse that's not occupied—and likely won't be occupied any time soon. Due to being sprayed so much by the water of Lake Erie during the winter of 2010, the lighthouse completely froze over. The lighthouse, which was built in 1910, was only used until 1965.

14. Eggshelland in Lyndhurst, Ohio is an Easter display that happens each year. Its constructed from thousands of hand-painted Easter eggs.

15. President Warren G. Harding's Home in Marion, Ohio is open to the public. Among the artifacts, you'll find there is a urinal, which contains some of his actual urine.

16. The African Safari Wildlife Park, which is located in Port Clinton, Ohio, lets you drive through the park to observe and feed the animals from your car. Unfortunately, no lions can be found at the park (for safety reasons, of course). So, what animals *can* you find in the park? Some of the animals you might encounter at the park include

giraffes, zebras, white zebras, buffalos, deer, camels, llamas, warthogs, alpaca, bison, elk, and more!

17. Longaberger Basket Building in Newark, Ohio is an office building that's shaped like a giant basket. It boasts itself as the "world's biggest basket." The building is considered a piece of artwork. It's been described to look like "a picnic basket in the middle of a field."

18. The Arnold Schwarzenegger Statue can be found in Columbus, Ohio. The Arnold Sports Festival, which is also called "The Arnold Classic," takes place in the city each year.

19. Neil Armstrong's First Flight Memorial can be found in Warren, Ohio. The site of Armstrong's first flight can be identified thanks to a replica of the moon landers.

20. The Troll Hole in Alliance, Ohio is home to almost 3,000 troll dolls. It was opened in 2014 by Sherry Groom, who holds the record for the largest troll dolls collection. If you're a fan of the *Trolls* movie and dolls, this is one Ohio attraction you won't want to miss out on.

Test Yourself – Questions and Answers

1. Which of Ohio's amusement parks appeared in an episode of *The Brady Bunch*, reviving nationwide interest in roller coasters?

    a. Kings Island
    b. Cedar Point
    c. Coney Island

2. Which of Ohio's amusement parks boasts itself as the "Rollercoaster Capital of the World"?

    a. Kings Island
    b. Cedar Point
    c. Coney Island

3. Colo, the first gorilla to be bred in captivity, was born at which of Ohio's zoos?

    a. The Cleveland Metroparks Zoo
    b. The Columbus Zoo
    c. The Cincinnati Zoo

4. Harambe was killed at which of the following zoos?

    a. The Cleveland Metroparks Zoo
    b. The Columbus Zoo
    c. The Cincinnati Zoo

5. Which museum is Balto's body located at?

    a. The Toledo Museum of Art
    b. National Museum of the United States Airforce
    c. The Cleveland Museum of Natural History

Answers

1. a.
2. b.
3. b.
4. c.
5. c.

CHAPTER FIVE

OHIO'S UNSOLVED MYSTERIES, URBAN LEGENDS, AND OTHER WEIRD FACTS

Have you ever wondered what unsolved mysteries have happened in Ohio? Do you know about some of the state's popular urban legends? Do you know what locations in the state are believed to be haunted? Have you heard about of the state's biggest tragedies? Some of these facts may shock you. Some of them will leave you with goosebumps. Some of them are just plain weird. Read on to find out more about some of the weirdest things that have happened in Ohio.

One of the Most Tragic Kidnapping Cases of All-Time Happened in Ohio

Chances are, you may have heard of the Ariel Castro kidnappings, which took place in Cleveland, Ohio. While this mystery has been solved, it's worth mentioning because it's one of the most tragic kidnapping cases to ever take place in the United States.

It all started out in August of 2002 when Michelle Knight went missing. Knight, who had been 21 years at the time of her disappearance, had been expected to appear in court over the custody of her son, who was in foster care. It was thought that Knight ran away due to losing custody of her son. Police didn't investigate her case as much as they might have otherwise due to a lack of tips and because she was an adult.

Amanda Berry went missing in April of 2003, the day before she turned 17 years old. Berry had let her sister know that she'd gotten a ride home from her job at Burger King. Although Berry was believed to be a runaway at first, the nature of the investigation changed after Amanda's mom had received a phone call from her daughter's cell phone. The caller was an unnamed man who said he had Amanda and that she was fine and would return home in a couple of days.

The following April, 14-year-old Gina DeJesus also went missing. The last person to see her was her friend Arlene, Ariel Castro's daughter. Arlene had called her mom, Grimilda Figueroa, to ask if Gina could spend the night. Figueroa had said no, and the girls had separated at the payphone. No one saw Gina DeJesus again.

All three girls accepted a ride from Ariel Castro and

were then lured into his house, where they were locked inside upstairs bedrooms, fed only one meal a day, and only allowed to use a toilet that wasn't changed often. He raped them and otherwise abused them, even going as far to beat Michelle Knight to cause her to miscarry five times after he'd impregnated her. Castro later forced Knight to assist in delivering Amanda Berry's baby, which he had fathered, in an inflatable pool. Castro had threatened to kill Knight if the baby didn't survive.

The Cleveland Police were able to connect Amanda Berry and Gina DeJesus's disappearances. The two girls were featured on *America's Most Wanted*, *The Oprah Winfrey Show* and *The Montel Williams Show*. On Montel Williams' talk show, so-called psychic Sylvia Browne had told Berry's mother that her daughter was dead.

In May of 2013, Ariel Castro left the house for the day. Amanda Berry managed to scream to his neighbors for help. After two of Castro's neighbors helped Berry and her six-year-old daughter escape the house, she ran to another neighbor's house to call 9-1-1. Police rescued Michelle Knight and Gina DeJesus from the house.

Castro was arrested the same day on four counts of kidnapping and three counts of rape. He was sentenced to life in prison without the possibility of parole.

Lots of UFOs Are Sighted in Ohio

UFO sightings are pretty common in the Buckeye State. In fact, Ohio ranks in at No. 9 for the states with the most UFO sightings, according to the National UFO Reporting Center. Since the center was established in 1974, there have been 3,473 reported sightings in the state. Hundreds of reported UFO sightings have taken place in Cleveland.

The most famous Ohio UFO sighting of all time is known as the "Portage UFO Chase." Back in 1966, two Portage County police officers were on the side of Route 224 when they saw a large disc-shaped UFO. The UFO flew right over their police cruiser and shined a bright light over them. The UFO hovered near them, but it moved whenever the officers tried approaching it. The officers chased the UFO into Pennsylvania. A formal investigation found that the officers were chasing a communication satellite and the planet Venus, which the officers found so insulting they quit their jobs. This incident got so much publicity that it even inspired a scene in the 1977 movie *Close Encounters of the Third Kind.*

It's also believed that a lot of UFO sightings take place over Lake Erie. People often see strange lights that change colors over Lake Erie. Known as the Cleveland Lights, they're often attributed to the NASA Glenn Research Center in Cleveland, which tests rockets and specialty aircraft. The U.S. Coast Guards have claimed the lights are the result of TV and radio towers or a windmill farm along the coast of Lake Erie. But people who live in the area aren't convinced by either of these explanations. Residents claim the lights don't look like a helicopter or plane. There have also been reports of the Cleveland Lights changing in color and brightness and moving up and down. The lights also disappear for months at a time. Seems kind of strange, if you ask me.

The Haunted Cedar Point Carousel Horse

Did you know that the *only* haunted carousel horse that's known to exist can be found at Cedar Point amusement park?

Known as Muller's Military Horse, the horse was carved by Daniel C. Muller back in 1917. There are several variations of how the carousel horse came to be haunted, but the most popular version of the tale goes like this: Muller's wife was so fond and protective of the horse that she didn't want anyone to photograph it. Rumor has it that Muller caught his wife cheating on him and murdered both her and her lover. He supposedly carved their bones into the horse.

While this story hasn't ever been verified, employees used to claim to see the ghost of Mrs. Muller riding the carousel horse. People also had a difficult time photographing the horse.

If you're worried about ending up on this haunted carousel horse when you're at Cedar Point, don't worry. The original carousel ride has since been moved to a different amusement park. Muller's Military Horse still remains at Cedar Point, but it's allegedly in storage. Some have claimed to sight the ghost of Mrs. Muller wandering the park in search of her carousel horse.

There is a replica of Muller's Military Horse at the Merry Go Museum in Sandusky, Ohio, which some people have claimed is also haunted.

The Lake Erie Monster

Did you know there may be a lake monster lurking around in one of Ohio's lakes? There have been many reported sightings of the lake monster, who has been nicknamed "Bessie" or "South Bay Bessie."

While people still report seeing Bessie in recent times, historical reports of the creature are far more common.

Reported sightings of the lake monster aren't entirely consistent. The monster is said to resemble a snake. Reports on the monster's length have varied, however, ranging from 16.5 to 40 feet in length.

The first reported sighting of Bessie in Ohio took place in Sandusky back in 1793. A captain of a sloop called *Felicity* allegedly startled the monster while he was duck hunting. He claimed the monster was 16.5 feet long.

In 1817, a crew aboard a schooner in Sandusky reported seeing Bessie, who they claimed was somewhere between 30 and 40 feet in length. In their report, Bessie was dark in color. The same year, another boat crew claimed they saw a 60-foot long monster, which they claimed was copper in color. They fired muskets at the monster, but it didn't kill it.

Later in 1817, French immigrant brothers in Toledo claimed they saw a "huge" monster on the beach. They claimed the monster was 20 to 30 feet long and resemble a sturgeon, except for one notable difference: this monster had arms. The monster, they claimed, appeared to be writhing in a way that appeared it was going to die. The brothers left the beach because they were afraid. When they returned, they found marks on the beach and silver scales, but the monster was gone.

Reports of Bessie sightings have continued until this day.

This leaves us with the question of why do all of these descriptions of Bessie not match up? Is it possible that there's more than one lake monster lurking in the depths of Lake Erie?

The Circleville Letter Writer

The Circleville Letter Writer is widely regarded as one of the creepiest, most chilling unsolved mysteries in the state of Ohio, if not the entire country. It's almost like a real life *Pretty Little Liars.*

Back in 1976, people who lived in Circleville, Ohio began to receive mysterious letters that contained personal information. Written in block style, the letters were mysterious, violent, revengeful, and even vulgar.

One Circleville resident, in particular, was affected by the mystery: a bus driver named Mary Gillespie. In his letter to Mary, the Circleville Letter Writer accused her of having an affair with the school superintendent. At the time, Mary denied the affair. The letter writer claimed that he (or she) had been watching Mary's house and knew she had children. A little over a week later, Mary got another letter. While there wasn't a name of who wrote the letters or anything more than "The Circleville Writer," both letters had been postmarked from Columbus, Ohio.

Mary didn't tell anyone about the letters at first, but then her husband, Ron Gillespie, got a letter, too. His letter came with a warning. The anonymous sender said Ron's life would be in danger if he didn't put a stop to his wife's affair.

Mary and Ron had their suspicions about who was sending them the letters. The only people they told about the letters were Ron's sister and his brother-in-law, Karen and Paul Freshour.

In August of 1977, Ron received a phone call from

someone who claimed to be the Letter Writer. The call allegedly infuriated him. He never told Mary who the caller was. Even though the caller supposedly claimed to be watching Ron's truck, he still grabbed his gun and left the house.

This was the last time Ron was ever seen alive.

Ron's body was found dead in his truck at an intersection close to where the Gillespie's lived. The truck had allegedly crashed into a tree, but only *after* a shot had been fired from his gun. One suspect was questioned, but authorities eventually ruled Ron's death an accident. Despite initially saying the death had been a result of foul play, Sheriff Radcliffe later claimed that Ron had been drunk at the time of the accident and had lost control of the vehicle. This outcome had come as a surprise since Ron allegedly rarely drank.

Shortly after, people who lived in Circleville began to get letters, too. This time, the letters claimed that Sheriff Radcliffe had covered up the accident.

Mary and the superintendent finally admitted to their relationship, but they said it didn't start until years after the Circleville Letters.

In 1983, the Circleville Letter Writer began to threaten Mary on her bus route, placing signs next to the road. When Mary went to rip down one of the signs, she found that it was a booby trap, containing a gun that was strategically placed in a way that could have fired at her if she had touched it the wrong way.

The serial number on the gun matched a gun that was owned by Ron's brother-in-law Paul Freshour, who had recently separated from his wife. However, Paul alleged that his gun had been stolen.

Paul was asked to take a handwriting test to see if his writing matched that of the letters. He was also asked to write the letters and repeat them verbally, as per Sheriff Radcliffe's request.

Sheriff Radcliff then asked to see where Paul kept his gun.

Paul was arrested for attempted murder the same day.

In October of 1983, Paul went to trial for attempting to murder Mary Gillespie. While no charges were brought against him for the letters, they were a part of the evidence used in the case.

Paul was the letter writer, according to the testimony of a handwriting expert. Mary testified that she believed Paul was behind it, too, after she'd received a visit from his wife who believed he was guilty. Paul's boss testified that he hadn't been at work the day Mary had found the booby trap, though Paul did have an alibi for the majority of that day.

Paul was found guilty and sentenced to seven to 24 years in prison.

If Paul was the one behind the letters, that meant they should have stopped during his incarceration... but they didn't.

The Circleville Letter Writer continued to send letters to people in the town, all of which were postmarked from Columbus, Ohio. But how could this be when Paul was in prison in Lima, Ohio?

At first, police believed that Paul was still somehow sending the letters while he was in prison. It was believed that he was somehow giving them to someone else, who would then mail the letters from Columbus. To find out for sure, they placed him in solitary confinement without any way of writing letters and constant monitoring. But people still continued to receive letters.

The prison warden said it was impossible that Paul could have been behind these letters. But he was still denied parole in 1990. The Circleville Letter Writer sent Paul a letter then, mocking him for this outcome.

In 1994, Paul was released on parole.

The Circleville Letter Writer has never been found.

When *Unsolved Mysteries* was filming an episode on the case, they received a postcard, too, warning them to forget Circleville and not to hurt Sheriff Radcliffe. The note warned that they "would pay." The letter was, of course, signed "The Circleville Writer."

If Paul didn't do it, then who did?

There are a couple of theories. Some believe that David Longberry, a school bus driver who worked with Mary Gillespie, wrote the letters because she rejected his romantic advances. In 1999, Longberry raped an 11-year-old girl and later committed suicide while he was a wanted fugitive. Others believe that Longberry may have written *some* of the letters, while Karen Freshour wrote the rest in a plot to frame her ex-husband.

Unfortunately, it doesn't look like the world will ever know who wrote the Circleville Letters.

The Mystery of Brian Shaffer's Disappearance

The disappearance of Brian Shaffer is one of the strangest unsolved mysteries in all of Ohio. In fact, the case is so baffling that it received national attention when it happened. Let's take a closer look at why.

In April of 2006, 27-year-old med school student Brian Shaffer disappeared after a night of bar hopping to kick off spring break with two of his friends, Clint Florence and Meredith Reed. The three went to Ugly Tuna Saloona, which is located in Columbus near Ohio State University. Meredith dropped them off at first and then later returned for the last call.

After they were there for a while, Shaffer ended up going off on his own, separating from his friends.

Florence and Reed called Shaffer in an attempt at finding him, but he didn't answer his phone. When the bar closed at 2 a.m., they went outside to wait for him before eventually deciding that he must have gone back to his apartment without letting them know.

No one has ever heard or seen from Brian Shaffer again.

His father and his girlfriend, Alexis Waggoner, tried calling him that weekend. Shaffer also didn't show up at the airport for a trip he and Waggoner had scheduled for spring break in Miami.

A missing person's case is weird enough in itself, but here's where things really start to get *really* weird. The bar only had one accessible entrance/exit, which were surveilled by security cameras. Shaffer was seen on camera talking two women before 2 a.m. He was then seen re-entering the bar. But no footage ever showed Shaffer exiting the bar again. Footage from security cameras at nearby bars also didn't catch Shaffer on camera, leaving investigators puzzled.

There are a number of theories on what happened to Brian Shaffer.

Some have wondered if foul play may have been involved in Shaffer's disappearance. Some suspicion was cast on his friend Clint Florence. Everyone who had interacted with Shaffer that night, including his father, had been asked to take a lie detector test. Florence, however, refused.

At one point, police theorized that the Smiley Face serial killer may have murdered Shaffer. The Smiley Face killer was believed to be a killer—or gang of killers—behind the murders of men whose bodies have been found in bodies of water. Not only have most law enforcement agencies—including the Columbus police—rejected the idea that the serial killer even exists, but Brian Shaffer's body hasn't been found to support these claims.

Others believe that Shaffer actually *chose* to disappear. He might have left the state, or even the country, in order to start a new life on his own. It's possible that he changed his clothes in the bar, put on a baseball cap, and kept his head down so no one would recognize him on the security cameras. To add fuel to this theory, his girlfriend Alexis continued to call his cell phone to listen to his voicemail for months after his disappearance. In September, his phone rang three times. The cell phone company said it may have been due to a computer glitch. Shaffer's phone wasn't GPS enabled, so it couldn't be located. People have also claimed to see Brian Shaffer in both the United States and Sweden.

Brian's own brother, Derek, believes his brother might still be alive. Derek Shaffer also believes that Clint Florence might know where he's located, which is why he's refused to take a lie detector test.

Alexis, however, doesn't believe that Brian would have just disappeared. She believes that her former boyfriend is dead.

The case was featured on a segment of *Dateline NBC* called "Into Thin Air."

The Disappearance of Louise Davis

In June of 1979, 17-year-old Evelyn "Louise" Davis went missing.

The day she went missing, Louise had been sunbathing in the yard with her mom. Louise's friend Darla's husband, Robert Wooten, came over to the house in East Liverpool, Ohio to talk to Louise. Wooten had allegedly told Louise that Darla had just returned from a trip she had taken and wanted to see Louise. Excited to see Darla, Louise left with Robert. Before Louise left, her mother had given her a curfew of 10 p.m.

Louise Davis never came home that night.

The following day, Louise's father and sister, Rachel, ran into Robert Wooten. When they asked him where Louise was, Robert told them she ran away and that they shouldn't wait for her to come back.

Louise's family reported her disappearance to Liverpool Township Police Department, who opened an investigation. They also began their own investigation, searching everywhere they could think of.

The family didn't believe Louise had run away from home. She had left $500 in her purse, makeup, and her toothbrush at home.

Four days after Louise went missing, Robert Wooten murdered his sister-in-law Debbie Taylor and two of her children.

Wooten confessed to the crime and is currently spending a life sentence on one count of murder and two counts of aggravated murder. He's incarcerated at Belmont Correctional Institution.

While most people believe that Robert Wooten is likely involved in Louise's disappearance, no evidence has been found that links him to the case. Wooten also denies any involvement.

However, a few weeks after Wooten confessed to murdering his sister-in-law and her children, the Liverpool Township Police Department received an anonymous letter. The letter stated that Robert had killed Louise. It also named a location where her clothes could be found.

When police arrived at the location, they found Louise's clothes.

Unfortunately, Louise's parents will never know the truth about what happened to her, as they both passed away in the 1990s. Her sister and cousin continue to search for her, though they both believe she is dead.

The case, which was featured on *Dateline NBC* in 2018, is still active.

Cincinnati Music Hall May Be Haunted

Did you know that Cincinnati Music Hall is said to be haunted? In fact, many believe it might be one of the biggest haunts in the *entire country*, and here's why: it's built on top of a burial ground.

Back in the 19th Century, a steamboat exploded in Cincinnati. The bones of people ended up getting scattered throughout the city. The skeletal remains of the victims were all placed in a field.

Cincinnati's first mental institution was then built on top of the field. When a cholera outbreak took place in the city during the 1830s, a lot of children were left orphaned. Some of the building was converted into an orphanage for those children, as well as a quarantine area for people who hadn't been affected by cholera. A lot of people died in the building, ranging from homeless people to suicide victims. Eventually, the building was demolished. The Cincinnati Music Hall was then built over it.

As the Music Hall was being built and later renovated, some disturbing discoveries were made. In 1927, more than 60 coffins were found on the property. In the

1980s, workers found a large pile of bones behind a concrete wall.

Since the 1980s, the Cincinnati Music Hall has been said to be a hotspot for ghost sightings. It has been said that the apparitions of people in viewing boxes have been seen waving, and the ghost of a boy dressed in 19th Century attire haunts the place. People have also claimed to feel cold air, hear strange knocking sounds, and hear music playing while the Music Hall is closed.

Hell Town Urban Legend

Some of the most popular urban legends in the state of Ohio involve Hell Town.

The area that's today known as "Hell Town" was once Boston Mills. The Boston Mills area was purchased by the United States government to build Cuyahoga Valley National Park. This meant they had to buy out the land from the people who lived in Boston Mills. This came as sudden, unexpected news to the residents, who weren't given any say in the decision. They weren't happy about being forced to move out. Some of them even compared it to how the Native Americans must have felt.

Once the Boston Mills residents left town, the government shut it down. The town's buildings were often set on fire for firemen training purposes. Over time, the former town of Boston Mills became a ghost town.

People have claimed that Boston Mill's remains can still be found within Cuyahoga Valley National Park. Abandoned buildings, guardrails, and some former roads apparently remain in the area, which hikers allegedly stumble on when they're inside the park.

There are a number of urban legends involving Hell Town. They include the following:

- It's believed that the government may have shut down Boston Mills in order to cover up a chemical accident that caused citizens to mutate. There have even been alleged reported sightings of disfigured, mutated people in the area.

- There's a church in the middle of Hell Town where satanic cult worshippers go. The church in question allegedly used to be a part of Boston Mills. There have been claims that the church has an upside-down cross.

- Hell Town is haunted by the spirits of murdered children. The tale goes like this: a school bus ran out of gas when it was passing through the area. The bus driver left to find gas, leaving the students on the bus unattended. At this time, a patient who had allegedly escaped from a nearby mental hospital (or, in some variations of the story, a serial killer) came onto the bus and murdered all of the children.

- Some believe the government closed Boston Mills because it was a hotspot for UFO or supernatural activity.

- It has been said that there's a possessed road that tries to kill people who try to drive its curves. While no one knows for sure if spirits are actually behind the accidents, there *are* a lot of car accidents in the area.

The Legend of the "Melon Heads"

The tale of the "melon heads" may sound really far-fetched, but it's another one of Ohio's most popular urban legends. The "melon heads" are said to be from Kirtland, Ohio.

The local legend goes like this: the melon heads were orphans who were cared for by Dr. Crow (or Crowe). Crow allegedly performed experiments on the kids, which caused them to develop large, bald heads and malformed bodies.

It has been said that the kids had hydrocephalus and that, as part of his experiments, Dr. Crow injected additional fluid into their brains.

Lore says that the kids then killed Dr. Crow, burned down the orphanage, and lived in the forests where they allegedly went on to feed on babies.

People have claimed to see the melon heads on Wisner Road in Kirtland, Ohio. Others have reported alleged sightings in Chardon Township.

A 2010 filmed called *Legend of the Melonheads* was based on the legend of the melon heads and other urban legends in Kirtland, Ohio.

The Disappearance of Beverly Potts

The disappearance of Beverly Potts is one of Cleveland's most well-known unsolved mysteries.

In August of 1951, Beverly, who was 10 years old, went to Halloran Park with a friend named Patricia to see an end-of-the-summer show. Her friend ended up leaving early. Prior to her disappearance, Potts was last seen walking toward the intersection of Linnet Avenue and West 117 around 9:30 p.m.

Children who were at the show and questioned about the incident had a number of stories. Several children had claimed to see Beverly leave with two men, but the colors of the cars didn't match up in their stories. When questioned about it, Beverly's friend Patricia claimed to remember seeing a strange woman stand behind Beverly and touch her shoulder. Although some have suggested that Patricia's memory might not have been good, others believe this is an important part of the case. While Beverly probably wouldn't have trusted a man well enough to leave with him, it's been suggested that she might have trusted a woman.

While it has been assumed that Beverly Potts was abducted and murdered, her body still hasn't been found. Multiple people have confessed to the crime, but many of them have been hoaxes. There was an anonymous tip about a potential suspect in 2015, but the case still remains unsolved.

As of 2018, Beverly Potts has been missing for 67 years. Sadly, even *if* the case is ever solved, her mother, father, and sister have all since passed away, so they will never know what happened to Beverly.

The Haunted Ohio State Reformatory

Did you know the Ohio State Reformatory, where the movie *The Shawshank Redemption* was filmed, is thought to be one of the most haunted spots in the state?

Today, there are guided tours and ghost hunts at the historical site, which is located near Mansfield, Ohio. It has been said that just setting foot in the place will make you realize how haunted it really is. People touring the facility have reported seeing shadows and hearing strange noises and even conversations.

Built in November of 1886, the Ohio State Reformatory served as an operational prison. It was for young, first-time offenders who could potentially be reformed, as a halfway point between the Boys Industrial School in Lancaster and the State Penitentiary in Columbus, OH. The reformatory operated until 1981, or for 94 years. During that time, a lot of violence, disease, and death took place in the facility.

The Ohio State Reformatory is believed to be haunted by several ghosts. One of the ghosts that are thought to haunt the former prison is that of Arthur Lewis Glattke, who was the prison warden between 1935 and 1959. His wife, Helen, is also thought to haunt the building.

Helen died in 1950 as the result of an "accidental shooting." She allegedly knocked a loaded gun off a shelf, causing a bullet to go through her lung. Many have questioned the circumstances surrounding her death. Some wonder if Helen may have committed suicide, while others have questioned if Arthur may have killed her. In 1959, Arthur himself died of a heart attack, which took place in his office a few years after Helen's death.

The ghosts of former inmates are believed to haunt Ohio State Reformatory. In 1955, one inmate hung himself. Another committed suicide by using turpentine and paint thinner to burn himself to death. Two inmates were cramped into a single solitary confinement cell once. The following morning, one was found dead, stuffed under the bunk.

There were also two correctional officers who died in the prison whose ghosts are believed to wander the halls. Those include an officer who was shot to death by a former inmate in 1926 and another officer who was beaten to death by a three-foot pole by an inmate in solitary confinement.

Due to all of these tragedies, Ohio State Reformatory is said to be a hotspot for paranormal activity.

The Ceely Rose House

The Ceely Rose House is located near Lucas, Ohio, on the land of Malabar Farm State Park. It's a working farm, but it has a haunting history. In fact, because of its history, some people consider the Ceely Rose House to be the most haunted place in Ohio.

The house was named after Ceely Rose, a teenager who lived in the house back in 1896.

Ceely Rose wanted to marry a local boy. However, her family didn't want them to get married. When her family didn't give their blessing, Ceely poisoned their cottage cheese with arsenic. Within weeks, Ceely's mother, father, and brother had all been found dead.

After admitting what she had done to a neighbor, Ceely Rose was committed to a mental institution. She died in the institution at age 83.

There have been reports of ghost-like voices and sightings of Ceely's apparition wandering through the hallways of the house. People have even claimed that Ceely's ghost has stared out at them through the window.

The Ceely Rose House has gotten so much attention that it was even featured on the TV show *Ghost Hunters*. The episode, which was filmed in 2014, is called "Family Plot."

The Ohio Prostitute Killer

Did you know that one of the most notorious serial killers in the state of Ohio still hasn't been found?

The Ohio Prostitute Killer is believed to be responsible for murdering at least eight prostitutes throughout the Buckeye State. The women were killed between the 1980s and 1990s. Their bodies were found along major interstates throughout the state. All of the victims were believed to be prostitutes who worked at truck stops.

The most famous victim was "Buckskin Girl," who was at first unidentified when her body was found in 1981. She was nicknamed after the buckskin jacket she'd been wearing at the time of her death. Her case was featured on an episode of *Unsolved Mysteries*, which connected her death to the mysterious prostitute killings throughout the state. DNA testing in 2018 found that the girl was a 21-year-old girl named Marcia King, who was originally from Little Falls, Arkansas. King's family had searched for Marcia, but they never reported her as a missing person.

It's believed that Marcia may have been the Ohio Prostitute Killer's first victim. The victims were all killed in a similar manner: they were strangled and had jewelry or clothing taken from them. Marcia, who allegedly wore no jewelry, did have her shoes removed.

So, who's behind these killings? One theory is that the killer may have been someone who went by the name of "Dr. No," a name he identified himself as over the CB radio. According to one of the victim's husbands, who was involved in his wife's sex work, a lot of prostitutes in the area found the man suspicious. "Dr. No" is believed to have been between 25 and 40 at the time of the killings.

To date, the Ohio Prostitute Killer still hasn't been caught.

The Haunted Franklin Castle

It has been said that Franklin Castle, which is a four-story mansion located in Cleveland's Ohio City neighborhood, is the most haunted house in the state. Built for German immigrant Hannes Tiedemann back in 1881, the house had more than 30 rooms, a ballroom, and a carriage house. But the house had secrets, too: secret passages, secret rooms, and secret sliding panels.

After Tiedemann's mother died, the family moved into the house. During their time living in Franklin

Castle, they buried four children, leading them to believe the house may have been cursed.

After Tiedemann's wife died during the early 20th Century, the house was sold. It was well-known at the time that the house held a dark, haunting history. There were rumors about incidents that had taken place in the home. One of the rumors was that Tiedemann had murdered his niece, his mistress, and a young servant in the home. However, no evidence of these alleged murders was ever found.

The Romano family came to own the Franklin Castle in 1968. Shortly after they moved in, the Romano family claimed there were strange things happening in the house, including ghostly encounters. Doors opened on their own, lights flicked on and off, and the sound of a baby crying could be heard throughout the house.

The Romano family also claimed that they saw the apparition of a woman in black. The woman was often seen staring out the front windows of the home.

The Romano family was so freaked out by these odd occurrences that they hired paranormal investigators and even an exorcist. But they ended up selling the house in 1974.

When Franklin Castle's new owner, Sam Muscatello, bought the home, he turned it into a haunted attraction.

Muscatello also began to try to uncover all of the house's secret passages. What he discovered was haunting. There was a pile of bones hidden behind a sliding panel in the tower. While the bones were never proven to belong to a human, they no doubt added to the overall darkness of the house.

Over the next 30 years, the house had several owners. A series of fires almost took the house down in 1999, but it managed to survive.

Franklin Castle is a private residence today. Those must be some brave homeowners.

RANDOM FACTS

1. Stark County, Ohio residents Bill and Dorothy Wacker were victims of harassment that began in 1984. They received strange, and at times threatening, phone calls. They were also robbed. The strangest part about the robbery was that their belongings were returned with written messages. Police believed the person behind the robbery had used their non-dominant hand to try to cover up their own handwriting. While the person behind the harassment has never been seen, it's believed that it was someone close to the Wacker family to have so much knowledge about their personal lives. Could the Circleville Letter Writer have been behind it?

2. Sandra J. Jenkins of Marietta, Ohio committed suicide back in 1911. A Macon, Georgia resident named Georgia Rudolph claims that she's Jenkins' reincarnated spirit. Rudolph says she's had weird visions about a woman in the 1900s. The visions began when Rudolph was just a child. These visions were so intense that Rudolph went to Marietta to find the house she believes she lived in during a past life, along with Sandra J. Jenkins' grandmother's grave. Then things took a strange

turn. A man said he was the reincarnated spirit of Sandra's boyfriend. To make things even creepier, he and Georgia both had some of the same visions about their past lives.

3. It has been said that Ohio State University is haunted by the ghost of Jeffrey Dahmer. The famed serial killer and cannibal attended the university for one semester, where he lived in "The Towers." If you were hoping to bump into the ghost of Jeffrey Dahmer at OSU, keep in mind that the story doesn't really line up. His ghost is said to haunt the residence hall where he lived, except... no one actually *knows* where Dahmer lived during his time at OSU. It may have been the Lincoln Tower, Morrill Tower or Drackett Hall. That being said, students are still convinced Dahmer haunts the dorms. Shrug.

4. Walhalla Road in North Columbus, Ohio is said to be haunted by the ghost of Dr. Mooney. Mooney, who lived on the road with his family, allegedly murdered his wife. It's said that his spirit reenacts the crime at night. In some of the legends, Dr. Mooney kicks his wife's severed head down the hill toward the road.

5. The tale of "Lizardman," or "The Loveland Frog," is based in Loveland, Ohio. Back in the 1950s, people claimed to see the Lizardman, a four-foot-tall humanoid that is said to be half man, half

lizard/frog. When the Lizardman waves a hand over its head, sparks allegedly fly to scare nearby people. The first appearance of the so-called Loveland Frog happened at 3:30 a.m. when someone claimed to see a group of the half human/lizard/frogs on the side of the road. Several police officers have also allegedly reported sightings of the Lizardman, but they've all changed their stories. It might sound like ridiculous folklore, but there have been recent sightings. In August of 2016, two teens in Loveland were playing Pokémon Go! when they claimed to see a giant frog that was walking on its hind legs.

6. "Gore Orphanage" in Vermillion is said to be one of the most haunted spots in Ohio. A fire once took place at the orphanage, causing dozens of young kids to burn to death. People who visit the orphanage have claimed they've heard children crying. There have also been sightings of apparitions and strange lights. The orphanage, which was actually named Light of Hope, was founded by husband and wife, Johann and Katharina Sprunger. They opened the orphanage in Vermillion after the two businesses they owned in Indiana also were taken down in flames. The children at the orphanage said the couple was abusive, neglectful, and even treated them like child slaves. Although there was an investigation

into the orphanage in 1909, there were no state regulations in place that could cause the couple's operation to be shut down. There's no actual evidence that any deaths took place at the orphanage, but it's still believed the place is haunted.

7. Rogue's Hollow, which is almost a ghost town in Ohio, is well known for its famously haunted "Crybaby Bridge." There are a couple of tales on why the bridge is haunted. The first story says that a woman threw her newborn baby over the side of the bridge and into the cold water because her lover left her. In another version of the legend, a couple got into an accident after hitting a patch of black ice on the bridge. The parents died instantly, while the baby died much later and cried for its parents until it died of starvation.

8. Staley Road in New Carlisle, Ohio is believed to be one of the most haunted streets in all of America. Although it might seem like a quiet street, it's also been home to a number of urban legends and strange encounters. The road's creepiness all stems back to a farmer whose surname was Staley, who the road was supposedly named after. Local lore says that Staley, who was the leader of a group of devil worshippers, killed his wife and kids in the family barn. Known as the "Bloody Barn," the formerly bright red barn (which has since been

painted gray) can still be found on the road. People have reported seeing the apparitions of children on the road, who are believed to be Staley's children. A number of other strange things happen on the road. Fog is said to often hang over the area. Car engines are said to die suddenly and unexpectedly. Cell phone batteries lose their power. Car accidents are also said to frequently occur on the Staley Road. Some of them are said to happen due to the barn, which is built really close to the edge of the road. Others happen around the bend of "Bloody Bridge." The cause of these accidents is said to be a figure that stands in the middle of the road. If you choose to travel this road, you might want to proceed with caution.

9. The Civic Theatre in Akron, Ohio is thought to be haunted. It has been said that the theatre is haunted by not just one but three ghosts. One of the ghosts is believed to be that of a janitor, who continues to clean the theatre even in spirit form. The second ghost who calls the theatre home is that of a young actor. This ghost has allegedly been caught haunting the balconies and backstage of the theatre. The third—and perhaps creepiest—ghost is thought to be that of a young woman who allegedly committed suicide by drowning herself in the canal the theatre was built on. Her apparition has been sighted in the underground of the theatre.

10. The Majestic Theatre in Chillicothe is said to be one of Ohio's biggest haunts. It has been said that a number of ghosts and spirits wander the wings of the theatre. However, the theatre's haunting history gives credibility to these claims. The theatre, which was built during the mid-19th century, was originally used as an opera house. In 1918, the Majestic served as a morgue when there was an outbreak of the Spanish Influenza at a military camp in the area. There was so much blood from the dead corpses in the alley next to the Majestic that people nicknamed it "Blood Alley." Today, people have claimed to see unexplained apparitions and fogs in the halls at the Majestic Theatre. The ghost of a young girl has been seen (and her giggles have been heard) backstage. Others have claimed to see the ghost of a man in a black suit walking the theater aisles. The apparition of a dead body was even allegedly seen onstage once during a performance.

11. Like many other states, Ohio has its own version of Bigfoot. Known as "the Grassman," this local folklore is said to be found near Minerva, Ohio. It's believed that stories of the Grassman date back to the 1700s, originating from the Native Americans. According to the Native American stories of this cryptid, it was 500 pounds, unfriendly, and walked on two legs. This sounds

much like the Grassman, who is said to be very aggressive. One family in the area claimed they were terrified by a group of Grassmen. Their dog was found with a broken neck and they found "Humanoid footprints" in their yard.

12. In July of 2002, an old man shot himself in an Eastlake apartment. He'd told everyone his name was Joseph Newton Chandler, except... it wasn't. When the authorities notified his next of kin, they were shocked to learn the real Joseph Newton Chandler had actually died in 1945. So, who was this man who'd stolen his identity? No one knows. Here's what we do know: he left behind $82,000 and electrical gadgets he'd designed, and he checked in a hospital in 1898 with severe penis lacerations. "Chandler" had claimed he'd gotten the lacerations from having sex with his vacuum cleaner.

13. Stivers School for the Arts in Dayton, Ohio is said to be haunted. The school, which opened in 1908, has a haunting past. Back in the 1920s, a teacher at school named Mary Tyler's body was found in the basement pool. Tyler had been holding a locket in one hand and a broken pointer in the other. Tyler had allegedly been involved with a student. The student, who had been a senior, disappeared after her body was discovered. He was never seen again. It has been said that his picture was in her

locket and he tore it out so he wouldn't be a suspect in the murder. The school ended up building a classroom on top of the pool, but a trap door still leads down to the pool. While the pool is only used for storage now, many believe Mary Tyler's spirit never left. Both students and staff have claimed to see Tyler's ghost levitating over the empty pool. There have also been reports of banging pipes and loud wails. In the classroom built over the pool, students have made claims of cool temperatures, disappearing objects, and flickering lights.

14. A human heart was once found in a Ziploc bag in a field near a gas station convenience store in Norwalk, Ohio. The bag, which was discovered by a pair of EMTs, contained a heart that was confirmed with 95% certainty to have belonged to a human. The eerie part is that no one ever figured out whose body the heart came from. Media outlets aired the story, but no bodies missing a heart were reported. At the time of its discovery, the heart was fresh. This means the heart had only just been removed from whatever body it came from. One possible theory is that the heart might have been lost in transit after an autopsy had been performed, but others suspect a serial killer who had meant to save the heart as a trophy.

15. The Butcher of Kingsbury Run, who has also been called the Cleveland Torso Murders, was believed

to be responsible for the murders of at least 12 homeless people in Cleveland during the 1930s. Most of the killer's victims were never identified. The serial killer got his name from the way he cleaved his victims' torsos in half. He also chopped off their heads. It's believed that the Butcher of Kingsbury Run might have also been behind the "Black Dahlia Murder," or the murder of Elizabeth Short. In 1980, a detective on the investigation claimed he was close to proving that a man named Jack Anderson Wilson was responsible for both the Torso Murders and the Black Dahlia Murder.

16. The residents of a small town called Defiance made reports of a werewolf in the summer of 1972. The people always claimed to see the werewolf during nighttime hours. Most of the sightings allegedly took place by the train tracks. The werewolf was described as huge, hairy, and wearing rags. While "the werewolf of Defiance" apparently left the town by the end of summer, people in the town still talk about it.

17. A 10-year-old girl named Amy Mihaljevic was kidnapped from a shopping plaza in Bay Village in 1989. A few days before Amy went missing, she had gotten a call from a man who claimed to be a friend of her mom's. The man asked Amy to meet him so he could go shopping with her to get a gift

for her mom. Amy wasn't the only girl in the area who had gotten calls from the man. Other girls who were from North Olmsted, like Amy. Another thing the girls all had in common was that they'd visited Lake Erie Nature and Science Center that autumn, where they had all logged their names. It's believed that's what may have linked them together. Some of the girls who had received phone calls were students of a math teacher who happened to be the brother of Amy's horseback riding instructor. The case remains unsolved.

18. In 1990, a 16-year-old girl named Lisa Pruett was found dead. She had been stabbed to death behind a mansion in Shaker Heights. Originally, Kevin Young, "the weird kid in school," had been the focus of the investigation. Young was even charged with murder, but he ended up being acquitted by a jury. Lisa Pruett's boyfriend, Dan Dreifort, has also been considered as a possible suspect. Pruett's body had been found stabbed to death approximately 100 feet from the Dreifort family's mansion on the *same day* Dan had been released from a psychiatric ward. While no evidence has linked Dan to the crime, he did write Lisa letters warning her to stay away from him once he got out of the hospital because he was afraid of hurting her. To make things even more

suspicious, it was Dan Dreifort's friends who told police that Kevin Young was responsible for the murder. To date, the case hasn't been solved.

19. In 1969, Ted Conrad was working as a vault teller at Society National Bank in Lakewood, Ohio. Conrad walked out of the bank one day with a brown paper bag, which was full of more than $200,000 in cash. Conrad disappeared without a trace, though he was later spotted in Hawaii.

20. In 2005, the body of 21-year-old Andrea Flenoury was found, wrapped in chains, in the river in Coventry Township, Ohio. She had been strangled to death. Flenoury had been working as a stripper at some of the shadiest clubs in town. Further investigation revealed that Flenoury was six weeks pregnant. Her killer has not yet been found.

Test Yourself – Questions and Answers

1. Which movie was inspired by an alleged UFO sighting in Ohio?

    a. Close Encounters of the Third Kind.
    b. 10 Cloverfield Lane
    c. The Fourth Kind

2. What is the name of the Lake Eerie Monster?

    a. Nessie
    b. Hessie
    c. Bessie

3. The area that's today known as "Hell Town" was once the town of ____.

    a. Boston Run
    b. Boston Mills
    c. Boston Valley

4. The name of the girl who escaped from Ariel Castro's home to call 9-1-1 was:

    a. Gina DeJesus
    b. Amanda Berry
    c. Michelle Knight

5. Ohio's Bigfoot is known as:

    a. The Grassman
    b. The Skunk Ape
    c. Dewey Lake Monster

Answers

1. a.

2. c.

3. b.

4. c.

5. a.

CHAPTER SIX

OHIO STATE
SPORTS FACTS

What do you know about Ohio's sports? Do you know which national sports league originated in the state? Do you know which popular ball was invented by a Cleveland businessman? Do you know which famous athletes come from the state? Read on to learn more about sports in the Buckeye State!

The Golf Ball Was Invented in Ohio

Did you know the modern golf ball was invented in the Buckeye State?

The modern golf ball was invented by Cleveland businessman and sportsman Coburn Haskell in 1898. The invention came about when Haskell was about to go on a golf outing with Bertram Work in Akron, Ohio. Bertram worked for the B.F. Goodrich Company. While Haskell was waiting in the factory for Work, he wound rubber thread into a ball. When the ball bounced, it almost hit the ceiling. Work gave Haskell the idea of putting a cover over the rubber thread and voila—the modern golf ball was born!

Haskell's design was known as the "rubber Haskell golf ball." He filed a patent for it in 1899. By 1901, he had retired from his job at M.A. Hanna Co. in order to start the Haskell Golf Ball Co. Haskell's invention soon went on to replace the gutta-percha ball, which was what had always been used to play golf prior to the rubber golf ball. Gutta-percha balls, which were made from dried sap from the Malaysian sapodilla tree. The rubber Haskell golf ball was a much more preferable option because it went a further distance. The new and improved technology helped to increase the popularity of golf.

And it all started out at B.F. Goodrich Company in Akron!

And a Legendary Golf Player is From Ohio!

With the modern golf ball being invented in Ohio, it seems fitting that a legendary golf player also hails from the state. Jack Nicklaus, also known as "The Golden Bear," was born in Columbus, Ohio.

Nicklaus raised in Upper Arlington, Ohio, where he attended Upper Arlington High School and participated in many sports. College basketball recruiters were even interested in him.

But golf was where his true talent lay. Jack Nicklaus began golfing at the age of 10. It was at Scioto Country Club where he played for the first time, scoring a 51 for the first nine holes he ever played.

Jack Nicklaus began to receive coaching at Scioto Country Club. Jack Grout, who often played with two famous professional players—Byron Nelson and Ben Hogan—ended up becoming Nicklaus's lifelong golf coach.

When he was 12 years old, Jack Nicklaus won his first Ohio State Junior title. He went on to win four more.

At 13 years old, Nicklaus broke a score of 70 at the country club. He became the youngest person to qualify into the U.S. Junior Amateur.

When he was 14, Nicklaus won the Tri-State High School Championship, where golfers from high schools in Ohio, Kentucky, and Indiana competed. Nicklaus finished with a score of 68. The same year, Nicklaus scored his first hole-in-one during a tournament.

At 15 years old, Nicklaus qualified for the U.S. Amateur. He won the Ohio Open when he was 16, where he competed against pro golfers and scored a 64 during the third round.

Between the ages of 10 and 17, Nicklaus won a total of 27 events throughout Ohio.

After high school, Jack Nicklaus went to Ohio State University. During that time, he won the U.S. Amateur two times, as well as an NCAA Championship.

In 1959, Nicklaus defeated champion Charles Coe. This was considered a miraculous defeat, partly because of Coe's previous undefeatability. It also made Nicklaus the youngest champion of the era. The only other champion who was younger than him had been Robert A. Gardner, who had won in 1909.

In 1961, Nicklaus set another record when he became the first golf player to win the individual title at the NCAA Championship *and* the U.S. Amateur during the same year. Only four other players (Phil Mickelson, Tiger Woods, Ryan Moore, and Bryson DeChambeau) would go on to achieve the same thing.

Nicklaus achieved his first professional win at a major championship at the 1962 U.S. Open. Nicklaus defeated Arnold Palmer by three shots, which sparked a feud between the two golf legends.

In 1966, Jack Nicklaus became the first golfer to win the Masters Tournament two years in a row. The same year, Nicklaus, who was 26 years old, became the youngest person to win the Open Championship.

During the course of his 25-year career, Jack Nicklaus won 18 Major Championships (the Masters Tournament, U.S. Open, Open Championship, and PGA Championship). He finished his career with 73 victories, which ranks him 3rd in all-time victories (finishing only behind Sam Snead and Tiger Woods). But to some, Nicklaus is still regarded as the best golf player of all time!

The NFL Started Out in Ohio

Did you know that the National Football League (NFL) started out in the Buckeye State?

The NFL was founded in September of 1920 at a meeting that took place at the Hupmobile Showroom in Canton, Ohio.

It might surprise you to learn that while the NFL was established in Ohio, professional football actually started out in Pittsburgh, Pennsylvania. In 1892, the Allegheny Athletic Association paid former Yale football star William "Pudge" Heffelfinger $500 to play *one* game.

Over the course of the next 30 years, pro football began to spread throughout western Pennsylvania and the Midwest. But there was just one problem: there was no sense of order. This is what led to the establishment of the NFL. The league, which was originally named the American Professional Football Association (APFA), made Jim Thorpe its first president. Thorpe was the most famous football player at that time, which helped give the-then APFA credibility.

At the meeting, there were representatives from eleven franchises: Canton Bulldogs, Akron Pros,

Decatur Staleys, Cleveland Indians, Daytona Triangles, Chicago Cardinals, Hammond Pros, Muncie Flyers, Rock Island Independents, Massillon Tigers, and Rochester Jeffersons.

By the time the first official season started in 1920, the Massillon Tigers had withdrawn from the league, choosing never to join the NFL. But by the time the season started, more teams had joined the league: the Chicago Tigers, Columbus Panhandles, Detroit Heralds, and Buffalo All-Americans.

Only two of the franchises that originally joined the NFL are still a part of the league today. Those are the Decatur Staleys, who moved to Chicago in 1921 and were renamed the Chicago Bears, and the Chicago Cardinals who are now the Arizona Cardinals.

And the First NFL Game Ever Was Played in the State!

Knowing the NFL started out in Ohio, it may come as no surprise to learn that the first game of the then-American Professional Football Association took place in the Buckeye State.

The first game was played on October 3rd, 1920 at Triangle Park in Dayton, Ohio. The game was played between the Dayton Triangles and the Columbus Panhandles. The Triangles beat the Panhandles by 14-0 at the Triangle's home stadium.

There were 4,000 people in attendance. They were charged $1.75 for admission to the game.

Lou Partlow, who was a running back for the Triangles, was the first to ever score a touchdown in the league. The touchdown was a 7-yard rush in the third quarter. A second touchdown was scored by Frank Bacon on a punt return. The extra points in the game were kicked by George "Hobby" Kinderdine.

The Dayton Triangles finished off 1920 with a strong season. They had 5 wins, 2 ties, and 2 losses. It was the best season the team had over the course of the next 10 years before finally being sold to Brooklyn in 1930.

Triangle Park no longer hosts games for the NFL, but you can still visit the park in Dayton today. It's currently used for other sporting events, recreation, and community gatherings.

The Dayton Sports History Center in Carillon helps preserve the city's NFL legacy. Established in 2012, the center is home to the Triangle's old locker rooms, which were restored prior to being added to the center.

The Pro Football Hall of Fame is in the Buckeye State

Did you know the Pro Football Hall of Fame is located in Canton, Ohio? You might be wondering how it ended up in Canton, of all places.

In the early 1960s, the people of Canton, Ohio campaigned for the NFL to build the Hall of Fame in their city. Canton was selected for obvious reasons: the NFL was founded there and the (now defunct) Canton Bulldogs were a successful NFL team when the league was first established.

The Hall of Fame, which opened back in 1963, helps preserve the history of football. The Hall of Fames enshrines—or inducts—NFL players, coaches, franchise owners, and front-office personnel. Players and coaches need to be retired for at least four years before they're considered for enshrinement. Between four and eight people are enshrined in the Hall of Fame every year. Once someone has been inducted into the Pro Football Hall of Fame, they remain an inductee forever.

Today, the Pro Football Hall of Fame is a popular Ohio tourist attraction. Hundreds of thousands of NFL fans travel across the world to visit the Hall of Fame—and for good reason. The Hall of Fame museum offers a number of exhibits and artifacts that would be of interest to NFL fans.

The Hall of Fame Gallery allows you to see the bronze bust of each inductee. There are touch-screen kiosks that allow visitors to explore the Hall of Famers' biographies, photographs, and video footage.

In, *the Pro Football Adventure Room*, you'll learn more

about the other professional football leagues that have been competition for the NFL since it was established.

In the *Moments, Memories & Mementos Gallery*, you'll learn more about the achievements that have been made by the Hall of Famers.

The *Pro Football Today Gallery* is filled with artifacts from recent record-breaking performances.

The *Lamar Hunt Super Bowl Gallery* will provide you with a recap of every Super Bowl in history. It's also home to the Super Bowl Theater, where you'll get to watch an NFL Films production.

There's also an interactive area in the museum where you'll find the Call-the-Play-Theater, a Teletrivia game, a Madden EA Sports video game display, and other fun exhibits.

The Hall of Fame store sells merchandise. Not only will you find merch that's specific to the Hall of Fame, but you'll also find merchandise for every team in the NFL.

The Pro Football Hall of Fame is also home to Tom Benson Hall of Fame Stadium. Everything from football games to lacrosse games and even concerts is held at the stadium throughout the year.

The Hall of Fame Game Happens in Canton, Ohio Each Year

Every year, the Hall of Fame Game, which is the yearly NFL preseason opening game, takes place at Tom Benson Hall of Fame Stadium. The game is generally held in August and officially jumpstarts the NFL preseason.

The Hall of Fame Game also kicks off Enshrinement Week. One of the Pro Football Hall of Fame's biggest draws, Enshrinement Week happens every year. More than 100 "Gold Jackets" (or returning Hall of Famers) attend the event each year. Fans are able to see and interact with the Hall of Famers. It's a popular time for fans to get photos and autographs of their favorite Hall of Famers.

There's also a Hall of Fame Parade which takes place during Enshrinement Week. Known as the Canton Repository Grand Parade, the parade is attended by the current Class of Enshrinees and Gold Jackets. You'll also see floats, helium balloons, animals, bands, and everything else you'd expect to see at a parade.

The First Ever Professional Baseball Team Was in Ohio

Did you know that Ohio was home to the first *ever* professional baseball team? Back in 1869, the Cincinnati Red Stockings became the first pro baseball team.

In 1869, the National Association of Base Ball Players (NABBP) made the decision to allow players to be paid. Harry Wright, an English-born baseball player, organized and managed the first professional baseball team—the Cincinnati Red Stockings, which had already been established three years prior.

Under Wright's management, the team had 10 salaried players, including Harry Wright's younger brother George Wright. George was considered the team's most valuable player. It's been said that he might have even been the best player of his time.

The first professional baseball game happened in May of 1869. The Cincinnati Red Stockings played the Great Westerns of Cincinnati. The Red Stockings won 45 to 9.

That season, the Cincinnati Red Stockings won a total of 57 games and lost none. The Red Stockings traveled great distances to play games, ranging from San Francisco to Boston. It has been said that no other team has ever played such a wide continental scope of games at a commercial level.

The following season and after 84 consecutive all-time wins, the Cincinnati Red Stockings lost 8 to 7 to the Brooklyn Atlantics, who they played in Brooklyn. They lost a total of six games that season. Although the Red Stockings remained one of the strongest teams, but their attendance began to decrease, especially at their home field.

The Cincinnati Red Stockings paved the way to baseball team uniforms and team names in the future Major League Baseball (MLB), which was established in 1903. The Red Stockings became trendsetters thanks to the continental scope of their baseball games, along with their overall success at the time. Red became the color of Cincinnati. The Cincinnati Red Stockings was named after their uniforms, which consisted of long red stockings. The Boston Red Sox later went on to name themselves after the team's style.

The Michigan-Ohio State Game is the Biggest Rivalry Game in College Football

Did you know that the biggest annual rivalry game in the history of college football takes place between the University of Michigan Wolverines and the Ohio State University Buckeyes?

The rivalry game has been played between the two state colleges almost every year since 1918. Since 1918, the location of the game has changed from Columbus, Ohio and Ann Arbor, Michigan, with Ohio State University hosting during even years and the University of Michigan hosting during odd years.

In 2000, *ESPN* named the game the "greatest North American sports rivalry."

If you're a fan of college football, then you may already know you don't need to travel to Ohio or

Michigan to watch the game. The game was aired on *ABC* for many years. As of 2017, *Fox* began to air the game.

Ohio's MLB Teams Have Won 7 World Series

Did you know that Ohio's Major League Baseball teams have won a total of seven World Series?

Five of those were won by the Cincinnati Reds, while two of them were won by the Cleveland Indians. The scores and dates were as follows:

1. 1919 – The Cincinnati Reds vs. the Chicago White Sox, 5-3

2. 1920 – The Cleveland Indians vs. the Brooklyn Dodgers, 5-2

3. 1940 – The Cincinnati Reds vs. the Detroit Tigers, 4-3

4. 1948 – The Cleveland Indians vs. the Boston Braves, 4-2

5. 1975 – The Cincinnati Reds vs. the Boston Red Sox, 4-3

6. 1976 – The Cincinnati Reds vs. the New York Yankees, 4-0

7. 1990 – The Cincinnati Reds vs. the Oakland Atlantics, 4-0

But an Ohio Team Has Never Won the Super Bowl

Despite Ohio's history in establishing the NFL, you might be surprised to learn that no NFL team from the state has ever won the Super Bowl. In fact, Ohio's two current NFL teams—the Cleveland Browns and the Cincinnati Bengals—are two of the 12 teams in the NFL who have never won a Super Bowl.

The Cincinnati Bengals made it to the Super Bowl back in 1981 and 1988. They lost both of those games to the San Francisco 49ers. The Cleveland Browns, on the other hand, have never made it to the Super Bowl.

A Legendary Basketball Player is From Ohio

Today, he's considered to be one of the best basketball players in the world and even one of the best basketball players of all time. Did you know that basketball legend LeBron James hails from Ohio?

LeBron James was born and raised in Akron, Ohio. James had a rough childhood. His mom was a single mother who struggled to find employment. As a result, she frequently bounced LeBron around from apartment to apartment in some of the less than desirable neighborhoods to live in. To provide him with a more stable home environment, LeBron's mom let him live with Frank Walker and his family. Walker, who was a local youth football coach, was the one who encouraged LeBron to play basketball, introducing him to the sport when he was just nine years old.

When he was a kid, James played for the Northeast Ohio Shooting Stars in the Amateur Athletic Union (AAU). James led the team to success at both the local and national level. He made friends with three other basketball players on the team, who called themselves the "Fab Four." They vowed to attend high school together. They ended up going to St. Vincent-St. Mary High School. The decision was a subject of controversy among locals, as the Catholic school was predominantly white.

LeBron James had a history of success and records that he set while playing basketball for St. Vincent-St. Mary High School's Fighting Irish basketball team. When James was just a freshman, he scored an average of 21 points and 6 rebounds during his freshman year. The team became the only boy's high school team to have an undefeated season. They also won the Division III state title under James' lead.

LeBron James' performance during his sophomore year earned him the title of Ohio Mr. Basketball, something that was previously unheard of for a 10th grader. The same year, he was also the first sophomore to ever be chosen for the *USA Today* All-USA First Team (which he would go on to do his junior and senior year as well, becoming the first in history to ever be chosen for three consecutive years).

As he was about to enter his junior year of high school, LeBron James was featured in *SLAM Magazine*, where he was said to possibly be "the best high school basketball player in America" at the time. During that basketball season, James also was featured on the cover of *Sports Illustrated*. He was the first high school underclassman to ever appear on the cover. James was also the first high school junior to be chosen as the Gatorade National Player of the Year.

While he was a high school senior, LeBron James was so popular that one of his games against Oak Hill Academy was aired nationally on *ESPN2*, and *Time Warner Cable* even had St. Vincent-St. Mary's games through pay-per-view. James' performance during his senior year earned him the Gatorade National Player of the Year again and Ohio Mr. Basketball for the third year in a row.

During his senior year, LeBron James was at the forefront of controversies regarding gifts. His mother gave him a Hummer H2 for his 18th birthday. She had only managed to get the vehicle by using his future NBA superstar earning potential. The Ohio High School Athletic Association (OHSAA)'s guidelines stated that high school players weren't allowed to accept anything more than $100 in rewards for athletic performances. After an investigation, it was determined that James hadn't broken any rules because the car had been given to him by family, rather than an agent. But then James accepted two jerseys that were $845 in value from an urban clothing retailer in exchange for modeling. It was determined that this was a violation of the OHSAA's rules. While James was initially stripped of his high school sports eligibility, he appealed the ruling and was just suspended for two games.

In 2003, LeBron James was drafted by the Cleveland Cavaliers. He was named NBA Rookie of the Year his first season.

By 2010, James had gone on to play for the Miami Heat and then went back to the Cleveland Cavaliers in 2014. In 2018, he signed on with the Los Angeles Lakers.

Over the course of his career, James has earned numerous awards, including three NBA Most Valuable Player Awards and two Olympic gold medals. He also currently holds the record as the highest scorer in the NBA playoffs.

A Famous Gymnast is From the Buckeye State

Did you know that one of the most famous gymnasts of all time hails from Ohio?

Simone Biles was born in Columbus, Ohio. Due to her single mother's drug and alcohol addiction, Simone and her siblings spent time in and out of foster care. In 2013, Simone and her sister were adopted by their grandfather, who was originally from Cleveland but lives in Spring, Texas. Simone's brother was adopted by their aunt.

While she was on a daycare trip in Texas, then six-year-old Simone Biles first got to try gymnastics. The gymnastics' instructors believed she should continue with it. When she was eight years old, Simone began training with Aimee Boorman at Bannon's Gymnastix in Houston.

Since then, Simone Biles has gone on to win four Olympic gold medals, giving her the American title of the most gold medals in women's gymnastics at a single Olympic event. Individually, Biles won the all-around, vault, and floor gold Olympic medals in 2016. Biles also won an Olympic gold medal as a part of the "Final Five," a gymnastics team that competed back in 2016. She also won a bronze medal for the balance beam as an individual.

And to think it all started out in Columbus, Ohio!

Roger Clemens Hails from Ohio

Did you know that former MLB player Roger Clemens was born in Dayton, Ohio? Clemens grew up in Vandalia, Ohio before moving to Houston, Texas, where he graduated from high school.

He began his baseball career with the Boston Red Sox. He later played for the Toronto Blue Jays, New York

Yankees, Houston Astros, and then finished his career out after playing his final season with the New York Yankees again.

Clemens was most recognized for being a hard-throwing pitcher, which was a tactic he used to intimidate batters. Many consider Roger Clemens to have been one of the best pitchers in the history of the MLB. And to think, it all started out in Dayton!

The Cincinnati Reds Betting Scandal

Pete Rose, who was known as "Charlie Hustle," was one of the best switch hitters of all time. Rose played for the Cincinnati Reds, Philadelphia Phillies, Montreal Expos, and the Cincinnati Reds again, from which he retired as a player in 1986.

During the course of his 23-year-long MLB career, Rose won three World Series, a Most Valuable Player Award, Rookie of the Year Award, two Gold Gloves, and three batting titles. He also broke a number of records, including all-time MLB player in hits (4,256) and games played (3,562).

His career came to a screeching halt in 1989 when he was working as a manager for the Cincinnati Reds. Rose was permanently banned from the MLB following allegations that he had gambled on baseball games while he was both playing and managing for the Cincinnati Reds. While Rose denied the allegations at first, he came forward in 2004 and confessed that he had bet on his own team.

In 1991, Rose was banned from the baseball Hall of Fame when they voted to ban "permanently ineligible" former MLB players from induction. Although Rose has petitioned the Hall of Fame to be inducted, he still remains ineligible.

Whether or not Rose should be reinstated or inducted into the Hall of Fame is a constant topic of debate among MLB players. It doesn't look like either of those things are going to happen any time soon, however.

Former NFL Player Archie Griffin is From Ohio

Did you know that former NFL player Archie Griffin is from Columbus, Ohio?

Griffin attended Eastmoor High School, which is today known as Eastmoor Academy, in Columbus. He played as a senior fullback on the high school football team. Today, Eastmoor Academy's football field is named the "Archie Griffin Field" in Griffin's honor.

After high school, Archie Griffin went on to play football for the Ohio State University Buckeyes. With the team, he won four Big Ten Conference titles.

Griffin set a couple of records during his college football career. He was the first—and remains the only—college football player to ever win the Heisman Trophy twice. Griffin was also the first college football player to ever start in the Rose Bowl four times.

Archie Griffin went on to play for the Cincinnati Bengals. The team made it to the 1981 Super Bowl while Griffin was playing for them, which the Bengals lost to the San Francisco 49ers.

RANDOM FACTS

1. NFL quarterback Russell Wilson, who plays for the Seattle Seahawks, was born at the Christ Hospital in Cincinnati, Ohio. In 2012, Wilson tied with Peyton Manning for the most passing touchdowns by a rookie. When he signed with the Seahawks in 2015, his $87.6 million contract made him the 2nd highest paid NFL player.

2. DeHart Hubbard, who was the first African-American to win an Olympic gold medal, was from Ohio. Hubbard, who was raised in Cincinnati, won the running long jump at the Summer Games in Paris in 1924.

3. Jesse Owens, who was raised in Cleveland, has been recognized as one of the most famous track and field athletes of all time. By 1936, Owens had earned four Olympic gold medals.

4. In 2000, the Columbus Blue Jackets were a National Hockey League (NHL) expansion team. Nine years later, Ken Hitchcock led the team to win the NHL playoffs for the very first time.

5. The Cleveland Indians have changed their names several times in the past century. In 1901, the MLB team was known as the Cleveland Blues and then

the Cleveland Broncos in 1902. In 1905, they wanted a new name and had a write-in vote. The name that was chosen, the Cleveland Naps, was in honor of their best player at the time: Napoleon "Nap" Lajoie. When Lajoie left the team in 1915, they became the Cleveland Indians, which they remain today. However, many believe the team should change its name due to the derogatory nature of the word "Indians."

6. The 1989 film *Major League* was about the Cleveland Indians. It was directed by David S. Ward, who was a long-term fan of the Indians. It might surprise you to learn that the movie wasn't shot in Cleveland. Instead, it was filmed in Milwaukee with the game scenes taking place at Milwaukee County Stadium. Over 25,000 Cleveland Indians fans appeared as stadium extras for the last game in the movie, which was double what Ward had been hoping for.

7. The Cleveland Cavaliers used to play at Richfield Coliseum in Richfield, Ohio for many years. Today, the team plays at the Quicken Loans Arena. Up until 2005, the arena was called Gund Arena, which was named after Gordon Gund, former owner of the Cavaliers. Gund had paid for the arena's naming rights.

8. The Cleveland Browns were the first NFL team who scored a two-point conversion. Two-point

conversions hadn't been adopted by the NFL until 1994. The Cleveland Browns managed to score one early in the season. The point was converted when Browns' punters Tom Tupa ran in a fake extra point when the team played against the Cincinnati Bengals. Tupa ended up scoring three two-point conversions that season, earning himself the nickname of "two-point Tupa."

9. The Cleveland Cavaliers could have been called the Cleveland Presidents. Before the team ended up with its name, the Cleveland Presidents, the Cleveland Jays, and the Cleveland Foresters were all considered.

10. Two of the Cleveland Cavaliers have earned the Rookie of the Year Award: LeBron James (2004) and Kyrie Irving (2012).

11. Former MLB umpire Billy Evans was raised in Youngstown, Ohio. Evans, who was known as "The Boy Umpire," was the youngest umpire in MLB history. He became an umpire when he was just 22 years old and officiated the World Series at 25 years old.

12. Former NFL player Dan Dierdorf is a Canton, Ohio native. Dierdorf played for the St. Louis Cardinals. Since his retirement, Dierdorf has worked as a sportscaster. He was most well-known for being a broadcaster for *Monday Night*

Football until 1999. In 2008, the Pro Football Hall of Fame awarded him with the Pete Rozelle Radio-Television Award.

13. Benny Friedman was a former NFL player. He played for the Cleveland Bulldogs, Detroit Wolverines, New York Giants, and Brooklyn Dodgers. Friedman was considered to be the leading NFL passer of his time. He was a star passer when he played between 1927 and 1930. He later went on to be the head coach for the New York Giants in 1930 and for the Brooklyn Dodgers in 1932. Friedman was a Cleveland native.

14. A number of well-known NASCAR drives are from Ohio. These include Frank Lockhart, Sam Hornish, Jr., Tim Richmond, Ted Horn, Bobby Rahal, and Mauri Rose.

15. A number of NASCAR events have been hosted at the Mid-Ohio Sports Car Course. Some of these include the CART World Series, NASCAR Xfinity Series, IndyCar Series, Can-Am, Formula 5000, American Le Mans Series, Rolex Sports Car Series, and ISMA GT Championship.

16. Miller Huggins, who was born in Cincinnati, was a former MLB player. He played for both the Cincinnati Reds and the St. Louis Cardinals. He later went on to manage the Cardinals and the New York Yankees.

17. Former NFL player Jack Lambert was born in Mantua, Ohio. Lambert played for Kent State University in Ohio before being drafted by the Pittsburgh Steelers.

18. The late NFL player and Hall of Famer Marion Motley has been called "the greatest all-around football player" in history. Motley, who was raised in Canton, was also one of the first African-Americans to play professional football in modern times. Motley attended Canton McKinley High School before eventually going on to play for the Cleveland Browns and Pittsburgh Steelers in the late 1940s through the mid-1950s.

19. Olympic women's hockey player Brianne McLaughlin is from Elyria, Ohio. She went to Elyria Catholic High School before going on to play for the United States women's national ice hockey team and the Buffalo Beauts in the National Women's Hockey League.

20. Olympic silver-medalist Bridget Sloan was born in Cincinnati, Ohio. The artistic gymnast won the 2009 world championship in the all-around and United States national championship.

Test Yourself – Questions and Answers

1. Which legendary basketball player is from Ohio?

   a. Magic Johnson
   b. Shaquille O'Neal
   c. LeBron James

2. The Pro Football Hall of Fame is located where?

   a. Canton, Ohio
   b. Dayton, Ohio
   c. Columbus, Ohio

3. Which former NFL player is _not_ from Ohio?

   a. Archie Griffin
   b. Russell Wilson
   c. Peyton Manning

4. The biggest college rivalry game of all time is between Ohio State University and _____.

   a. Indiana University
   b. The University of Michigan
   c. The University of Akron

5. Which ball, in its modern form, was invented in Ohio?

   a. The football
   b. The baseball
   c. The golf ball

Answers

1. c.

2. a.

3. c.

4. b.

5. c.

OTHER BOOKS IN THIS SERIES

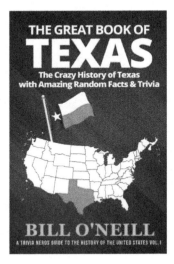

Are you looking to learn more about Texas? Sure, you've heard about the Alamo and JFK's assassination in history class, but there's so much about the Lone Star State that even natives don't know about. In this trivia book, you'll journey through Texas's history, pop culture, sports, folklore, and so much more!

In The Great Book of Texas, some of the things you will learn include:

Which Texas hero isn't even from Texas?

Why is Texas called the Lone Star State?

Which hotel in Austin is one of the most haunted hotels in the United States?

Where was Bonnie and Clyde's hideout located?

Which Tejano musician is buried in Corpus Christi?

What unsolved mysteries happened in the state?

Which Texas-born celebrity was voted "Most Handsome" in high school?

Which popular TV show star just opened a brewery in Austin?

You'll find out the answers to these questions and many other facts. Some of them will be fun, some of them will creepy, and some of them will be sad, but all of them will be fascinating! This book is jampacked with everything you could have ever wondered about Texas.

Whether you consider yourself a Texas pro or you know absolutely nothing about the state, you'll learn something new as you discover more about the state's past, present, and future. Find out about things that weren't mentioned in your history book. In fact, you might even be able to impress your history teacher with your newfound knowledge once you've finished reading! So, what are you waiting for? Dive in now to learn all there is to know about the Lone Star State!

GET IT HERE

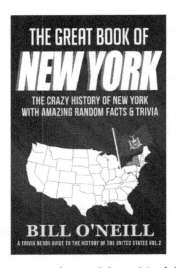

Want to learn more about New York? Sure, you've heard about the Statue of Liberty, but how much do you really know about the Empire State? Do you know why it's even called the Empire State? There's so much about New York that even state natives don't know. In this trivia book, you'll learn more about New York's history, pop culture, folklore, sports, and so much more!

In The Great Book of New York, you'll learn the answers to the following questions:

- Why is New York City called the Big Apple?

- What genre of music started out in New York City?

- Which late actress's life is celebrated at a festival held in her hometown every year?

- Which monster might be living in a lake in New York?

- Was there really a Staten Island bogeyman?

- Which movie is loosely based on New York in the 1800s?

- Which cult favorite cake recipe got its start in New York?

- Why do the New York Yankees have pinstripe uniforms?

These are just a few of the many facts you'll find in this book. Some of them will be fun, some of them will be sad, and some of them will be so chilling they'll give you goosebumps, but all of them will be fascinating! This book is full of everything you've ever wondered about New York.

It doesn't matter if you consider yourself a New York state expert or if you know nothing about the Empire State. You're bound to learn something new as you journey through each chapter. You'll be able to impress your friends on your next trivia night!

So, what are you waiting for? Dive in now so you can learn all there is to know about New York!

GET IT HERE

Are you interested in learning more about California? Sure, you've heard of Hollywood, but how much do you really know about the Golden State? Do you know how it got its nickname or what it was nicknamed first? There's so much to know about California that even people born in the state don't know it all. In this trivia book, you'll learn more about California's history, pop culture, folklore, sports, and so much more!

In The Great Book of California, you'll discover the answers to the following questions

- Why is California called the Golden State?

- What music genres started out in California?

- Which celebrity sex icon's death remains a mystery?

- Which serial killer once murdered in the state?

- Which childhood toy started out in California?

- Which famous fast-food chain opened its first location in the Golden State?

- Which famous athletes are from California?

These are just a few of the many facts you'll find in this book. Some of them will be entertaining, some of them will be tragic, and some of them may haunt you, but all of them will be interesting! This book is full of everything you've ever wondered about California and then some!

Whether you consider yourself a California state expert or you know nothing about the Golden State, you're bound to learn something new in each chapter. You'll be able to impress your college history professor or your friends during your next trivia night!

What are you waiting for? Get started to learn all there is to know about California!

GET IT HERE

MORE BOOKS BY BILL O'NEILL

I hope you enjoyed this book and learned something new. Please feel free to check out some of my previous books on Amazon.

IF YOU LIKED THIS BOOK, I WOULD REALLY APPRECIATE IF YOU COULD LEAVE A SHORT REVIEW ON AMAZON BY CLICKING HERE.